FAMILY ESTRANGEMENT

A HEALING WORKBOOK

FOR ADULT CHILDREN
TO BUILD BOUNDARIES,
RECLAIM PEACE,
AND MOVE FORWARD
WITHOUT RECONNECTION

FAMILY ESTRANGEMENT

A HEALING WORKBOOK

FOR ADULT CHILDREN
TO BUILD BOUNDARIES,
RECLAIM PEACE,
AND MOVE FORWARD
WITHOUT RECONNECTION

Amber Zahra

To those who were called selfish for setting boundaries,

dramatic for speaking the truth,

and cold for choosing peace.

May this be the space where your voice returns to you —

— and your healing becomes your own.

Disclaimer

This workbook is intended as a reflective and supportive tool for adult children navigating the emotional, relational, and personal complexities of family estrangement. It is not a substitute for professional mental health care, therapy, legal advice, or crisis intervention.

The prompts, exercises, and tools included are designed to foster insight, empowerment, and emotional healing. They are not meant to diagnose, treat, or replace the guidance of a qualified mental health professional. Every estrangement journey is different, and readers are encouraged to adapt the content to suit their own values, capacities, and lived realities.

If you are experiencing acute emotional distress, trauma symptoms, or feel unsafe, please seek support from a licensed therapist, counselor, or local mental health resource. If you are in immediate danger, contact emergency services or a crisis helpline in your area.

This workbook does not cover all possible dimensions of estrangement, including those involving abuse, legal action, systemic oppression, or cultural violence. These pages are meant to be a gentle companion, not a comprehensive solution.

Some examples in this workbook are inspired by real stories but have been adapted, fictionalized, or anonymized to protect individual privacy.

Use this workbook at your own pace. Take what serves you. Leave what doesn't. And return when you're ready.

Acknowledgments

To the brave souls who opened these pages while carrying stories too heavy to name—this book is for you.

To every reader learning to live with grief that has no rituals, family ties that fray instead of hold, and holidays that echo more than they celebrate—you are not alone.

To the mental health professionals, peer support facilitators, and trauma-informed listeners who make room for hard truths without judgment—thank you for modeling compassion that heals.

To my creative collaborators, early readers, and those who encouraged me to write what often goes unsaid—your belief in this book mattered more than you know.

And to those learning that self-protection is not betrayal, that silence can be sacred, and that healing doesn't need a witness to be real—thank you for walking this road with me.

Amber Zahra

Table of Contents

Introduction 11

Part I. Entering the Healing Space 13

1. You Get to Be Seen 15

2. Your Story, Your Voice 19

Part II. The Emotional Earthquake 23

3. Guilt and Shame — Breaking the Rules 25

4. Grief and Relief — A Loss Without Death 29

5. Anger and Betrayal — When Forgiveness Isn't the Goal 39

6. Lonely, but Not Alone 43

Checkpoint 1. Honoring What You've Faced So Far 47

7. Sadness, Doubt and Numbness 53

8. Fear and Anxiety — The What Ifs 59

Part III. What Was Never Your Fault 65

9. Family Roles — The Cast You Didn't Choose 67

10. Trauma Responses — Fawn, Freeze and FOG 73

11. Emotional Flashbacks — When the Past Floods In 79

12. Self-Gaslighting — Undoing the Doubt Spiral 85

Checkpoint 2. Reclaiming What Was Always Yours 89

Before you turn the page 93

Part IV. Building Boundaries, Identity and Protection 95

13. Rebuilding Self-Worth 97

14. Boundaries That Hold 101

15. Digital, Social and Legal Safety 105

16. When You've Been Cut Off 109

Part V. Life After the Break 113

17. Milestones Without Family 115

18. Triggers and Setbacks 119

19. Healing Isn't Linear 123
Checkpoint 3. Witnessing the Spiral 127
20. Chosen Family and Real Belonging 131
PART VI. Your Future Is Still Yours 137
21. Forgiveness and Your Timeline 139
22. Closure Without Their Words 143
Checkpoint 4. The Ending You Get to Write 147
Appendix A. Scripts for Real Life 154
Appendix B. Safety and Legal Planning 160
Appendix C. Cultural, Religious and LGBTQ+ Support 165
Appendix D. Myth vs. Reality 169
Appendix E. Glossary of Emotional and Trauma Terms 173
Appendix F. The Language of Healing 179
Appendix G. Letters You Will Never Send 182
Final Word from the Author 188
About the Author 191

Introduction

This is a place for truth and gentleness.

Family estrangement doesn't always begin with a bang.

Sometimes, it happens in a quiet fade — one unanswered message at a time.

Other times, it's brutal and fast. A door slammed. A word too sharp to unhear.

For some, it's chosen. For others, it's forced.

This workbook was made for all of it.

It's for the adult child who walked away to survive.

For the one who was pushed out and told they were the problem.

For the one stuck in an on-again, off-again loop, afraid to stay, afraid to go.

For the one who feels too guilty to talk about it and too ashamed to heal.

Estrangement is not just the absence of contact.

It's the ache of being unseen, unheard, misunderstood — or miscast into a role you never asked to play.

It's the grief that comes without funerals. The sadness that follows even relief.

It's the strange, quiet loneliness of losing people who are still alive.

You may still love the people who hurt you.

You may still question your decision.

You may have a hundred versions of the story in your head, and still not know what really happened.

This workbook won't force you to reconcile.

It won't tell you forgiveness is a requirement.

It won't ask you to "just move on."

It will not shame you for your choice — or your pain.

What it *will* do is help you rebuild from the inside out.

It will walk with you through the messy parts — guilt, anger, confusion, grief — without rushing you toward a perfect ending.

It will give you tools to feel safe in your body, clear in your boundaries, and grounded in your truth.

There is no single timeline for healing, and no right way to feel.

Whether your estrangement is brand new or decades old, there's space for your story here.

You do not have to justify your pain.

You do not have to explain your boundaries.

You do not have to pretend this doesn't hurt.

You're here — and that's a beginning.

This is your space to feel, reflect, and reclaim.

Start wherever you are. It's more than enough.

Part I. Entering the Healing Space

Before you begin this journey, you deserve something that may have been missing for a long time: permission to take up space.

Part I is your foundation. These first chapters are not about fixing anything. They are about offering you a soft landing. This is where you get to exhale, gather your bearings, and begin gently. You'll find tools to support emotional safety, clarity, and choice from the very first page.

This part of the workbook includes guidance on how to move through it at your own pace, along with practices that can anchor you in moments of overwhelm. You'll also be invited to map your story—not for anyone else's approval, but so you can begin to see your experience with clearer eyes and deeper compassion.

This is not a performance. This is not a test. You do not need to be "ready."

You only need to begin from where you are.

1. You Get to Be Seen

This workbook is designed to support *your* process—not dictate it. There is no required pace, no "right" way to begin, and no expectation to complete it in a certain order.

You will need a personal notebook or digital journaling tool to complete the exercises. This book does not include lined pages, by design. Your thoughts, experiences, and reflections deserve space beyond a fill-in-the-blank format.

Each chapter includes:

- Reflection prompts
- Somatic (body-based) grounding practices
- Cognitive tools (reframes, decision maps, self-dialogue)
- Optional letters or rituals
- Gentle encouragement and trauma-informed language throughout

You may choose to:

- Move through the chapters in order
- Skip ahead to a topic that resonates today
- Revisit certain sections as often as needed

There are no grades. No gold stars. Just space for truth and recovery.

Take what serves you. Leave what doesn't. You are not behind. You are exactly where your healing begins.

Before you begin: Safety tips for triggering sections

Because estrangement is emotionally complex, you may find yourself feeling overwhelmed, anxious, numb, or activated while reading certain parts of this book. That is not a failure. That is a trauma-informed signal—your body protecting itself.

To support yourself as you work through this material, consider the following:

- **Pause often** to check in with your body. Ask yourself: *Am I feeling present? Grounded? Safe?*
- **Keep soothing tools nearby**—whether that's a warm drink, a blanket, a calming object, or a grounding playlist
- **Do not push through distress**. Skip ahead, close the book, or return later. Stopping is a form of self-respect
- **Use movement**, even gentle movement (walking, stretching, shaking out your arms) to support your nervous system
- **Identify a support person** or resource (a therapist, friend, support group, or crisis line) in case you need connection

There is no benefit in retraumatizing yourself for the sake of progress. Healing is allowed to be kind.

Grounding practice: 5-4-3-2-1 — You're safe here

This is a simple, reliable tool to help return to the present moment when you feel emotionally flooded, frozen, or disconnected.

Begin by naming:

- *Five* things you can see
- *Four* things you can feel through touch
- *Three* things you can hear
- *Two* things you can smell
- *One* thing you can taste

Take a slow, steady breath in. Then exhale longer than you inhale.

You are here.

You are safe enough.

You do not need to rush.

2. Your Story, Your Voice

Before healing can happen, we often need to name what we've been through—not to explain it to others, but to *witness it ourselves*.

This chapter invites you to place your story in front of you, piece by piece, with gentleness and honesty. You are not expected to have a tidy summary of your estrangement. You might still be in it. You might not remember all the details clearly. You may carry conflicting truths. That's okay.

This is not about justifying your decisions. It's not about reliving trauma.

It's about *gathering the thread of your own voice*—the one that may have been buried under guilt, fear, loyalty, or silence.

You don't need to tell everything.

But you deserve to tell something.

And you deserve to tell it in your own words.

Estrangement timeline mapping

Use the following prompts to begin outlining key events that shaped your experience. There's no right or wrong amount of detail. Focus on what feels significant to you.

Start here:

- The earliest memory where something felt off, unsafe, or misaligned
- A moment when you felt invisible, dismissed, or pressured to stay silent
- A major event (conflict, betrayal, absence) that shifted the relationship
- The moment you considered distancing or cutting contact

- What followed—immediate relief, doubt, grief, pressure, silence?
- Any patterns that repeated: *"This happened again when..."*

You can draw this as a line, a series of waves, or write it as a bulleted list.

You do not need to make sense of everything. You only need to name what you remember.

What happened, and what still echoes

Take a moment to reflect on what you carry from this experience—even now.

Consider the following:

- What words still echo in your mind, even if you wish they didn't?
- What behaviors or dynamics still haunt your relationships with others or with yourself?
- What do you avoid talking about, even in safe company?
- What would you want to say out loud, just once, if it were safe to say it?

You can respond in list form, phrases, or even fragments. There is no need for polished sentences. Raw and real is enough.

Letter to Self: *This is how I've survived*

Write a letter—not to them, but to yourself. The part of you that kept going. The part of you that lived through the tension, the silence, the confusion, the grief.

You can begin with:

Dear me,

Here's what I've never been told enough:

Use this letter to:

- Honor the choices you've made
- Acknowledge the pain you endured
- Name the ways you adapted or protected yourself
- Thank the version of you that kept surviving, even when it hurt

You can keep this letter private. Tear it up, re-read it, or return to it later.

But write it like your truth matters—because it does.

Part II. The Emotional Earthquake

Grief doesn't always look like crying.

Anger doesn't always look like shouting.

Sometimes, pain settles into your body like static—tight shoulders, clenched jaw, an ache you can't name.

Sometimes, it shows up as guilt you can't shake, or a fear that keeps you scanning every room, every silence, every message.

Part II is about making space for the emotional aftershocks of estrangement.

You may be carrying grief for a parent who is still alive. You may feel anger that frightens you, or guilt that was planted in you long before you had a choice. You may feel relief and sadness at the same time—and wonder what that says about you.

You are not wrong for how you feel.

In the chapters ahead, you'll be invited to explore the emotional weight of estrangement with gentleness and honesty. These feelings are not signs of weakness. They are evidence of survival.

You don't need to rush through them. You only need to begin where you are.

This is where you learn to listen to your emotions without being ruled by them.

This is where we begin to name what still hurts—and why that makes sense.

3. Guilt and Shame — Breaking the Rules

Estrangement often doesn't feel like freedom right away. It feels like guilt.

Guilt for not calling. Guilt for protecting your peace. Guilt for not showing up to family events.

Shame for being "the one who left." For needing space. For drawing boundaries that no one else understood.

For many adult children, the guilt didn't start at estrangement. It began much earlier—when love was tied to performance, approval, obedience, or silence. When your value was measured by how well you could keep others comfortable. When you learned to disappear, so others didn't have to look at their own pain.

If you feel guilty, it doesn't mean you did something wrong.

If you feel ashamed, it doesn't mean you are wrong.

This chapter is about disentangling guilt from wrongdoing—and shame from identity.

Guilt is a feeling. It doesn't always point to truth.

Shame is a wound. It doesn't get to define who you are.

Let's begin with what you were taught.

Cultural and inherited shame inventory

Before you examine your current guilt, it may help to identify the unspoken rules you were raised under. These are often reinforced by culture, faith, gender roles, or family hierarchy—and rarely questioned until you begin to heal.

Reflect on the following statements. Which ones were modeled, taught, or expected in your family or culture?

- *Family loyalty comes before personal happiness.*

- *You must honor your parents, no matter what they've done.*
- *Good children keep the peace, even if it hurts them.*
- *You don't speak about private matters outside the family.*
- *Love means staying, even when it's painful.*
- *Forgiveness is a moral obligation.*
- *You owe your parents your time, money, or presence.*
- *Cutting off family is selfish and unforgivable.*
- *Disrespect means saying "no."*

Now, take a moment to name your own:

- What belief, spoken or unspoken, kept you trapped in guilt?
- What did you fear would happen if you stopped performing those roles?
- What cultural or religious narratives added weight to your choice to distance?

Write freely in your personal notebook. It's okay if this stirs discomfort. That's not failure—it's a sign that the story is shifting.

Guilt reframe tool

In your personal notebook, draw two columns.

Label the left column: *"What I feel guilty for"*

Label the right column: *"What I was actually doing"*

Here are a few examples to guide you:

- *I feel guilty for not answering my mother's calls → I was protecting my peace after repeated emotional harm*
- *I feel guilty for skipping the family reunion → I was honoring a boundary that kept me emotionally safe*

- *I feel guilty for setting limits on my time → I was prioritizing my own mental health*

Now create your own list of 5 to 10 examples.

Then ask yourself:

- Was I doing harm—or finally honoring my own needs?
- Is this guilt based on love, fear, or programming?

Sometimes guilt is just a sign that you've started living differently.

Compassion practice: It wasn't your job to keep them happy

Take a moment to say this sentence aloud—slowly, even if it feels strange:

"It wasn't my job to keep them happy."

Let that settle in your chest. Again:

"It wasn't my job to keep them comfortable at the cost of my own pain."

Breathe.

This practice is not about blame. It's about unburdening. If you were trained to regulate everyone else's mood, your nervous system may associate guilt with safety. But you are not responsible for the unhealed wounds of those who raised you.

You may still love them. You may wish things had been different.

But *you do not have to keep abandoning yourself to prove your love.*

In your notebook, complete the sentence:

"It wasn't my job to..."

List as many truths as you can.

Example:

- It wasn't my job to fix their marriage.
- It wasn't my job to manage their emotions.
- It wasn't my job to stay silent to keep peace.
- It wasn't my job to disappear.

***

You are not a bad person for needing boundaries.

You are not selfish for saying no.

You are not wrong for feeling guilt that isn't yours to carry.

Healing doesn't mean you'll never feel guilt again.

It means you'll learn to tell the difference between *real responsibility* and *learned obligation.*

You were never meant to carry the weight of everyone else's happiness.

You were meant to live a life rooted in truth.

And you're allowed to begin doing that now.

4. Grief and Relief — A Loss Without Death

Grief has a way of showing up quietly after estrangement.

Not always as tears. Not always as sorrow.

Sometimes as a lump in your throat when you hear a song.

Sometimes as guilt on a birthday you didn't acknowledge.

Sometimes as a strange ache when the phone doesn't ring—*even though you asked for distance.*

What makes this grief especially complex is that it's often wrapped in relief.

You might feel freer, lighter, more stable.

And yet, you still mourn something.

Maybe not the relationship as it was—but the one you wish it could have been.

This chapter is about making space for both truths:

You can feel relieved, and still feel sad.

You can grieve someone who caused harm.

You can miss someone, and still not want them back.

This doesn't mean you're confused. It means you're human.

Unsent letters to family

One way to process unresolved feelings is to write a letter you will never send.

This is not a letter for *them*. This is a letter for *you*—a space to release what's been held in silence, shame, or fear. It can contain anger, longing, confusion, gratitude, sorrow, or all of the above.

You can begin with any of the following openers:

- *I wish you knew...*
- *You never asked, but here's what I would have said...*
- *This is what I carried when I walked away...*
- *I loved you, and I still needed to leave...*
- *I miss parts of you, even now...*
- *I deserved more than what you gave...*

There's no need to write a full letter in one sitting. Add to it over time. Or write many. You can tear them up, keep them, burn them, or reread them only when you're ready.

The point is not to be heard. The point is to let the truth leave your body.

Example Letter: If you were cut off by a parent

Dear Dad,

I don't know if you'll ever think of me the way I still think of you.

When you stopped calling... when the silence stretched on... I told myself it was temporary. I made excuses for you. I waited for a message that never came.

At first, I felt erased.

Then I felt ashamed — like maybe I did something I couldn't remember, or failed some invisible test.

I replayed old conversations, searching for the moment everything broke. I wanted to believe this was just a phase. I wanted to believe you still saw me as yours.

But the truth is, I don't think you ever saw all of me.

Not the part that disagreed.

Not the part that hurt.

Not the part that stopped trying to please you.

I don't know if you distanced yourself because I changed — or because I stopped hiding the ways I had already changed long ago.

But the silence?

It said more than words ever did.

I still wish you had said something.

Even if it was hard. Even if we didn't agree.

But you left me to make meaning out of nothing. And it hurt.

I'm learning now that your silence was not my failure.

That your absence says more about you than it does about me.

That grief can live beside self-respect.

I don't need you to explain yourself anymore.

I just needed to say this.

Even if you never hear it, I do.

— Me

Reflection prompts

If you were cut off by a parent:

Use your personal notebook or journaling app to reflect on the following:

- What emotions surfaced as you read this letter — anger, sadness, guilt, numbness?
- Have you blamed yourself for their silence? Where did that blame come from?
- What do you wish you could say to them without needing them to agree?

- When did you first realize the relationship might be slipping away — and how did you respond?
- What part of yourself felt most rejected or unseen?
- How has their absence impacted how you see yourself today — and what do you want to reclaim?
- What would a letter of release, not reconciliation, look like for you?

***

If you were the one who stepped away

Sometimes healing means making the choice they never thought you would.

Maybe you held on for years.

Maybe you kept trying, hoping they would hear you differently this time.

Maybe you swallowed your pain, justified their behavior, or convinced yourself it wasn't *that bad.*

And then something shifted.

Not necessarily a blow-up — but a quiet clarity:

I can't keep doing this.

If you were the one who chose distance — from a parent, stepparent, or guardian — this is your invitation to write what couldn't be said.

Use your personal notebook or journaling app to begin. Here's one possible opening:

Letter Opener:

> *Dear Mom,*
>
> *I didn't leave because I stopped caring.*

I left because I kept disappearing.

For a long time, I tried to be what you needed — quiet, agreeable, grateful, invisible.

But I couldn't keep losing myself to keep the peace.

I know you might see my distance as betrayal.

But for me, it was survival...

(Continue writing in your own words.)

Reflection prompts

If you were the one who stepped away from a parent:

- What boundaries were you forced to break in order to protect yourself?
- What did it cost you to stay — and what has it cost you to leave?
- What feelings still surface when you think about your decision — guilt, grief, clarity, fear?
- If you weren't trying to be "fair" or "reasonable," what would you say without editing?
- What do you miss — and what do you not want to return to?
- Are there parts of you still seeking their approval, even in silence?
- What does choosing yourself look like today?

***

If it was a sibling or extended family member

Estrangement grief isn't always about parents. Sometimes, it's about the one who was supposed to ***understand****.*

You might have thought this person would always be there.

Maybe they were your ally once — or maybe they always stayed neutral while you broke open.

Sometimes estrangement happens slowly, in looks that avoid, messages left unanswered, or years of being made to feel like the problem.

This kind of grief is layered: it's not just the loss of *them*, but the loss of what you thought you had — or hoped you could build.

If this speaks to your story, consider writing a letter to that sibling, cousin, aunt, or relative. Start here if it helps:

Letter opener:

Dear Sister,

I didn't think it would be you.

You were supposed to be the one who saw it too — who knew what it was really like in our family, even when no one said it aloud.

But over time, the silence between us got louder than the truth we used to share.

Maybe you didn't mean to take their side.

Maybe it wasn't even about sides for you.

But it felt like you disappeared when I needed you to stay...

(Continue your version in your own notebook or journaling space.)

Reflection prompts

If your grief centers around a sibling or extended family member:

- What did this person represent for you — safety, validation, shared truth, or something else?
- When did you first feel the distance growing between you?

- Have you tried to explain your side to them — or have you carried the silence instead?
- What do you wish they could have said, done, or stood up for?
- How did family roles affect your connection with them?
- If you let go of needing them to understand, what would healing look like for you?
- What are you grieving most — the person, the bond, or the version of yourself who trusted them?

If you need more inspiration, turn to Appendix G: Letters you'll never send — and return to it anytime you're ready.

The goodbye that never came (Ritual ideas)

Estrangement often lacks closure. There is no funeral. No ceremony. No community support.

Just a quiet distance that stretches into months or years.

If you were never given a chance to say goodbye, you can create your own ritual now—not to erase the pain, but to acknowledge it.

Here are some ideas you can adapt to your needs:

1. Write and release:

Write a short message on paper to the person you're grieving. Fold it, tear it, or burn it safely. Say aloud: *"I release what I cannot carry anymore."*

2. Plant something:

Bury a small object, flower, or letter as a symbolic goodbye. Let new growth mark your healing.

3. Light and silence:

Light a candle in the evening. Sit with the flame and name what you are grieving. You can whisper, write, or simply feel.

4. Empty chair practice:

Place an empty chair in front of you. Imagine saying what you were never allowed to say. When finished, say: *"You no longer get to take space in my silence."*

5. Music and memory:

Create a playlist of songs that help you process your feelings. Allow yourself to feel what comes up without judgment.

You are not silly for needing a ritual.

You are not weak for needing a goodbye.

You are giving your grief the dignity it was denied.

Reflection prompts: What do I still miss—and why?

Use the following reflections in your personal notebook:

- What specific parts of the relationship do I miss (if any)?
- Is it the person, or the idea of who I wanted them to be?
- Do I miss the role I played—or how I imagined things could've been?
- What do I wish someone could have said or done to honor the ending?

Try to avoid censoring yourself. It's okay to miss them. It's okay to not miss them. It's okay to feel both in the same breath.

Grief after estrangement is not a mistake. It's a continuation of love, truth, and unmet hope.

***

Estrangement can feel like a death no one brings flowers to.

But your pain is real. Your sadness is valid. Your need to mourn is not dramatic—it's human.

You're allowed to say goodbye in your own way.

You're allowed to carry both the ache and the clarity.

And you're allowed to heal without pretending it didn't hurt.

If grief is the ache that lingers, anger is often the fire underneath it. In the next chapter, we'll explore the part of you that still wants to be heard — even if no one is listening.

5. Anger and Betrayal — When Forgiveness Isn't the Goal

Anger is often the most misunderstood part of the estrangement process.

You may have been taught that anger is dangerous. That it's ugly. That it means you're bitter or immature or holding a grudge. Especially if you are someone who was conditioned to be the peacekeeper, the "good one," or the one who absorbed everyone else's pain.

But anger is not the enemy. Suppressed anger becomes shame, anxiety, illness, disconnection. *Expressed* anger—safe, grounded, and truthful—is often the beginning of clarity.

This chapter isn't about getting over it. It's about getting honest.

You may never receive an apology. The harm may never be acknowledged.

But that doesn't mean your pain isn't real. And it doesn't mean you have to bypass your rage in order to appear healed.

Forgiveness is not the goal here.

Self-respect, safety, and truth are.

Anger tracking chart

Use this reflection tool to get curious about your anger instead of shaming it. In your personal notebook, create three columns with the following prompts:

1. When did I feel the angriest?

Describe the moment, memory, or trigger. Be specific if you can.

(Example: "When they called me selfish for not coming home for the holidays.")

2. What boundary was crossed?

What value, emotional limit, or physical space was violated?

(Example: "I had clearly said I couldn't afford the trip and they pressured me anyway.")

3. What message did my anger want to deliver?

Imagine your anger speaking clearly. What is it trying to tell you?

(Example: "I deserve to say no without being punished.")

You might begin to see patterns: repeated moments where your boundaries were not respected, where your voice was silenced, or where your needs were ridiculed.

This is not just "family conflict." This is the body remembering betrayal.

Somatic Tool: Punch Pillow or Scribble Page

When anger builds with no place to go, it can become internalized. This can show up as headaches, chest pressure, muscle tension, fatigue, or numbing behaviors. The body needs a way to release that energy—without causing harm.

Here are two safe options:

1. **Punch Pillow**

- Use a couch cushion, towel, or firm pillow.
- Find a private space where you feel safe.
- Set a timer for 1–2 minutes.
- Allow your body to move—punch, push, press—while breathing out tension.
- Afterward, rest your hands on your body and repeat: "It's safe to release."

2. **Scribble Page**

- Take a blank page and a pen or marker.
- Without overthinking, scribble as forcefully or freely as needed.
- You can write a word, draw lines, or press hard into the paper.
- Let the paper hold what your body cannot.

You are not "too much."

You are not overreacting.

You are responding to injury that deserves validation.

Let your body move what your words cannot.

Reflection: What boundary did they cross—again and again?

Use these prompts in your notebook to identify the recurring violations you endured—not to dwell in them, but to affirm that your anger has context.

- What specific boundary did they cross more than once?
- How did I try to express that it wasn't okay—and how was I met?
- What did I internalize because no one listened?
- What do I wish I had said—or screamed—at the time?
- If I had believed my anger was justified, what would I have done differently?

Your answers may surprise you.

Sometimes the betrayal wasn't one big moment—it was *a hundred small ones* that you were expected to swallow.

Anger is not just about them. It's about reclaiming *you*.

***

You don't need to forgive someone who has never taken accountability.

You don't have to soften your rage to make others more comfortable.

You don't owe anyone your silence just because they share your blood.

Anger is not what breaks you—it's what wakes you.

Let it speak. Let it move. Let it clear space for your truth.

6. Lonely, but Not Alone

Loneliness after estrangement is one of the most under-acknowledged emotional weights survivors carry. It doesn't just show up during quiet nights or family holidays. It can appear in a crowded room. During a celebration. On a regular Tuesday afternoon.

It's not just the absence of people.

It's the ache of being disconnected from a part of your history—even if that history was painful.

It's the silence where a call used to come, even if that call brought tension.

It's the longing to be known in a way that once felt familiar, even if it also hurt.

Estrangement can feel like a forced exile from a language only your family spoke—even if that language was made of sharp edges.

This chapter is about meeting your loneliness with truth and tenderness.

Not to "fix" it or deny it—but to learn how to live with it differently.

Prompt: When do I feel most alone?

In your personal notebook, reflect on the following:

- What situations bring up the strongest sense of loneliness?

(Example: holidays, illness, good news with no one to call)

- What emotions come up alongside that loneliness—grief, resentment, shame, confusion?

- Are there physical symptoms I feel when I'm lonely?

(Tight chest, foggy thinking, stomach pain, fatigue?)

- What do I usually do in response—withdraw, numb, overwork, seek connection?
- When was the last time I felt truly connected, even if briefly?

Understanding your loneliness doesn't make it disappear.

But naming it helps break the silence it thrives in.

Holiday loneliness plan

Holidays and family-centered events can feel like emotional landmines.

You're not imagining it—our culture often centers family as the default structure for belonging. When you're estranged, it can feel like the world is celebrating what you no longer have.

You don't have to pretend you're fine.

But you also don't have to surrender to dread.

Use the following plan to prepare for an emotionally charged time:

1. Anticipate the trigger

- What event, date, or tradition feels especially hard?
- What stories do I tell myself around it?

2. Create a compassion statement

Write one sentence you can repeat during the day:

"This ache is real, but so is my right to peace."

"I don't need to perform joy to belong in this world."

3. Choose one grounding activity in advance

- Take a long walk
- Journal or cry without interruption

- Watch something comforting
- Prepare food that nourishes you

4. Decide if you want connection or solitude—and plan for it

- Reach out to a friend?
- Plan a virtual call?
- Join an online space where estranged adults gather?
- Or, block time for being alone on your terms?

5. Debrief afterward

Note what helped, what hurt, and what you want to do differently next time.

You are allowed to rewrite the meaning of these dates.

You are allowed to *opt out*, create new rituals, or do nothing at all.

Tool: Mapping chosen connection

When you lose family connection, it can feel like all safety nets have been cut. But healing includes remembering this: *You are allowed to build new circles.*

In your notebook, try this mapping exercise.

Draw a circle in the center of the page. Label it "Me."

Now begin adding names around it—not just people, but:

- Friends who listen without judgment
- Coworkers or neighbors who feel emotionally safe
- Pets or animals who bring comfort
- Online communities or spaces where you feel seen

- Spiritual practices, music, books, or art that soothe and ground you
- Future spaces you hope to find connection in (yes, even hoped-for ones count)

Draw lines connecting these to you. Some may be thick, strong lines. Others may be light and tentative. That's okay.

Then reflect:

- Which connections nourish me now?
- Which ones need tending, expanding, or redefining?
- What kind of connection am I craving most?

Chosen family may not erase the ache of biological loss.

But it can offer something else: connection rooted in consent, care, and truth.

***

Loneliness after estrangement is real—and it is survivable.

It does not mean you made the wrong choice. It means you're human.

You may still long for connection. You may still miss what never truly existed.

But you are not alone in that longing.

There are others walking the same quiet road.

And with time, new paths of connection can be built—paths that begin not with pretending, but with *permission to be exactly where you are.*

And sometimes, after the ache of loneliness comes something even harder to name — the moments when you feel nothing at all.

Checkpoint 1. Honoring What You've Faced So Far

After grief, guilt, anger, loneliness, and survival — a pause to breathe

You've made it through the first part of this journey — not just by reading, but by staying with yourself in feelings many people spend a lifetime avoiding.

Let's name what you've walked through:

- Guilt that was never yours to carry.
- Grief without a grave.
- Anger you weren't allowed to express.
- Loneliness you thought you had to endure quietly.
- Emotional echoes from people who said they loved you, but couldn't show it safely.

This isn't light work. It's the kind of healing that rewires your nervous system, reframes your memories, and softens the self-blame you once thought was truth.

Maybe you've cried.

Maybe you've gone numb.

Maybe you've had moments where you questioned whether this kind of healing is even worth it.

Pause here, and let yourself acknowledge this:

You've already begun to reclaim your story.

Not by fixing the past, but by refusing to disappear inside it.

This checkpoint is a space to breathe, not to push forward.

It's a moment of gentle noticing.

Reflection prompts

(Use your own notebook or journaling app.)

1. What feelings have surprised you the most so far — and which ones feel familiar?
2. When have you noticed your body tightening, bracing, or shutting down while reading or reflecting?
3. What is one truth you've allowed yourself to admit — even if it's hard?
4. What would it mean to offer yourself *recognition*, not just resilience?
5. What do you wish someone else would say to you — and can you say it to yourself, even just once?
6. What belief are you starting to question — and what new belief is beginning to form in its place?
7. Where in your life are you already choosing healing, even if no one sees it?

Progress tracker — Checkpoint 1

You've just moved through some of the hardest emotional terrain: guilt, grief, anger, and loneliness. This tracker isn't about being "done." It's a way to witness how you're beginning to see yourself — and your past — with new clarity.

Use your personal notebook or journaling app to reflect. There's no right pace. Only honesty.

1. How do I feel about my family story — right now?

Write one sentence or phrase that reflects your current state.

Example: "Still conflicted, but clearer on what hurt."
Your words: ______________________________

2. What emotions are most present for me today?

Choose or add your own.

☐ Grief

☐ Anger

☐ Shame

☐ Numbness

☐ Sadness

☐ Relief

☐ Tiredness

☐ Other: ____________

3. What truth have I let myself acknowledge — maybe for the first time?

Even a whisper counts.

"I didn't deserve what happened."

"I wasn't the problem."

"It wasn't my job to fix everything."

4. What role did I used to play in the family — and how am I beginning to unlearn it?

Write one or two sentences.

Example: "I was the peacekeeper. I'm learning I don't have to make everything okay for others to be safe myself."

5. What's something I used to blame myself for — that I now see differently?

"Not speaking up."

"Walking away."

"Feeling angry."

6. Where have I already shown up differently — even if no one else noticed?

This might be:

- The way you set a small boundary
- The way you spoke to yourself during a hard moment
- The way you let yourself feel something without pushing it down

Write it down: ______________________________

7. Gentle self-message for this moment:

Write a sentence or two to your present-day self. Something kind. Something real.

"You're doing the hardest part — staying with yourself."

"You don't need to explain your pain to make it valid."

"This is healing. Even now."

Before you turn the page

This isn't weakness. It's what courage looks like up close.

You've just sat with some of the hardest truths — guilt that was planted in you, grief without clarity, anger you were never allowed to voice, and the silence of being unseen.

That deserves a pause. A breath.

And maybe even a small moment of recognition:

You stayed.

You showed up for the part of you that used to disappear.

But the emotional weight doesn't always lift just because we've named it.

Sometimes, it turns into something else — a dull ache, a fog, a sense of emotional exhaustion that's hard to name.

Sometimes it feels like everything at once — or nothing at all.

In the next chapter, we'll explore those in-between emotional states.

Not the loud feelings — but the quiet ones that sneak in after the storm: *numbness, doubt, emotional fatigue, deep sadness.*

The moments when it all feels too much — or like nothing matters at all.

You don't have to move through those feelings alone.

Let's keep going — gently.

7. Sadness, Doubt and Numbness

Not all pain is loud.

Some pain disappears into silence.

You go through the day flatlined. No tears, no rage—just a kind of emotional static. You're not okay, but you can't quite access what's wrong. You move through tasks. You answer messages. You say, "I'm fine."

This is often how sadness hides.

And how numbness protects.

After estrangement, it's common to swing between feeling *everything* at once... and then suddenly, *nothing at all*. You might feel sadness so heavy it makes your limbs ache. Or you might feel so detached it's like you're watching your life from outside your body.

You might wonder:

- *Why am I still so sad if I made the right choice?*
- *Why can't I feel anything at all?*
- *What's wrong with me for being like this?*

This chapter isn't here to pull you out of those feelings.

It's here to sit beside them—and help you understand what they're trying to say.

When sadness comes in waves

Sadness isn't always about what happened. Sometimes it's about what never did. The hug you needed. The apology that never came. The conversation that will never happen. The birthday that still hurts even if you didn't want to call.

You may feel sadness around:

- The relationship you hoped to have
- A parent who couldn't or wouldn't change
- The time you lost trying to be "good enough"
- How estrangement changed other relationships (siblings, grandparents, traditions)

This sadness may not be constant. But when it comes, it often asks to be *felt*, not fixed.

In your notebook, complete the following reflection:

- *What have I lost that I never truly had?*
- *What parts of myself still ache for connection—even if I know it's unsafe?*
- *What is this sadness asking me to honor, mourn, or let go of?*

You may not find neat answers. That's okay.

Sadness doesn't always arrive with clarity—but it deserves a seat at the table.

Prompt: What does numbness protect me from?

Now let's shift to the other common side of this chapter: emotional numbness.

For many estranged adult children, numbness is not failure. It's *protection*. It's how your nervous system kept you functioning when emotions were too much to feel all at once.

Numbness often shows up when:

- You've been emotionally overloaded for too long
- You're expected to "move on" while you're still in pain

- You're afraid to reconnect with feelings that were never allowed in the past

In your personal notebook, reflect on the following:

- *When do I feel emotionally "blank" or checked out?*
- *What situations tend to trigger numbness?*
- *If this numbness had a voice, what would it say it's protecting me from?*
- *What emotions might be under the numbness, waiting until it's safe to come forward?*
- *How did my family respond to sadness, tears, or emotional needs when I was younger?*

Let this be a place of curiosity—not judgment.

Numbness is not proof that you don't care.

It's often proof that *you've cared too much, for too long, without enough space to process it.*

Gentle movement for emotional release

When sadness or numbness lingers in the body, words may not be enough. The body holds emotion through tight shoulders, clenched jaws, shallow breath, stomach knots. To begin shifting this energy, movement can be more effective than thinking.

You don't need to go to a class or "do it right." These practices are about connection—not perfection.

Try one of the following today:

1. Rocking (seated or standing)

- Sit comfortably or stand with feet firmly on the ground.

- Slowly sway side to side, front to back, or in small circular motions.
- Wrap your arms around your body as if offering comfort to a younger version of you.
- Breathe into the movement. Let it calm your system.

2. Shoulder and arm touch

- Use your opposite hand to gently trace circles or strokes over your shoulder and arm.
- Switch sides.
- This gentle touch can awaken sensation when you feel emotionally numb.

3. Ground pressing

- Lie on the floor or bed and feel the surface supporting your body.
- Press your feet gently into the ground.
- Press your hands into your thighs or against a wall.
- With each breath, whisper: "I am here."

4. Scribble or shake practice

- Take a pen and scribble freely across a page. Or gently shake out your limbs—arms, legs, shoulders.
- Let the movement be messy, irregular, imperfect.
- The point is not to look a certain way. It's to *move what's stuck.*

Even five minutes can make a difference. You don't have to feel better.

You just have to feel *a little less trapped.*

Reassurance: You're not weak — You're navigating something most people never talk about

Feeling too much isn't a flaw.

Feeling nothing isn't a failure.

You may not cry when you think you should.

You may feel distant from your story, your body, or people who care.

You may go through the motions, numb and flat, and question whether this will ever change.

Let this be your reminder:

- You're not weak — you're navigating something most people never talk about.
- You are adapting.
- You are protecting something sacred—until it's safe enough to feel again.

Healing doesn't always look like growth.

Sometimes it looks like stillness. Sometimes it looks like surviving without knowing how.

Sometimes it looks like sitting with a sadness that has no words yet.

You are not failing.

You are healing in the only way you can right now—moment by moment.

8. Fear and Anxiety — The What Ifs

What if I made a mistake?

What if they come back and I cave?

What if I regret this one day?

What if I really *am* the problem?

Fear after estrangement is common—but it rarely gets named aloud. It can feel like a constant whisper in the background of your mind, replaying old conversations, projecting worst-case scenarios, and keeping you stuck in cycles of doubt.

This fear is not irrational. You were likely raised in an environment where boundaries were punished, emotions were dismissed, or safety was unstable. Anxiety becomes a way to prepare for the next emotional blow—before it ever arrives.

This chapter is here to help you slow the spiral.

To gently question the fears that haunt you.

To build safety from the inside out—even if it wasn't modeled for you.

You are allowed to be afraid.

You are also allowed to create a life that isn't ruled by fear.

Safety planning (emotional, physical, digital)

Estrangement sometimes comes with unexpected escalations: threatening messages, digital harassment, public shaming, or smear campaigns. Even if your situation hasn't involved this, the fear that it *could* happen can be paralyzing.

Let's create your three-tier safety plan—not from paranoia, but from self-trust.

1. Emotional safety plan

Use this to ground yourself during emotional overwhelm:

- *What signs tell me I'm emotionally triggered or spiraling?*

  (e.g., racing thoughts, shallow breath, zoning out, nausea)

- *What calms me when I feel unsafe or anxious?*

  (e.g., certain music, sensory tools, grounding exercises, movement)

- Who are my emotional anchors?

  (List people, communities, or helplines where you feel seen)

- What is my self-reminder during fear spikes?

  (e.g., "I can survive hard feelings without abandoning myself.")

2. Physical safety plan

For those experiencing harassment, stalking, or trauma triggers:

- *Do I need to limit in-person exposure to certain people or places?*
- *Is my home and physical space secure?*

  (Locks, privacy, security system, boundaries with neighbors)

- *Do I need backup support for certain events or situations?*

  (e.g., a support person at a family gathering, a check-in text)

3. Digital safety plan

Estranged family members sometimes use digital means to maintain control or guilt:

- *Have I reviewed my privacy settings on social media?*
- *Do I need to block, mute, or unfollow certain contacts?*

- *Is my personal information protected (address, photos, email)?*
- *Can I create a digital boundary statement to use when contacted?*

(e.g., "I'm not available for contact at this time. Please respect my space.")

Your nervous system will relax when it knows you have a plan. Even if you never need it, having it can be part of reclaiming peace.

What if...? Thought distortions and CBT challenge

Anxiety loves the phrase *"what if."* It uses it to keep you stuck in mental rehearsal and imagined doom.

Let's look at some of the most common "what if" fears that arise during estrangement—and gently challenge them.

In your notebook, write down the ones that apply to you. Then complete the reframes below or add your own.

1. What if I regret this later?

→ Regret is possible—but so is relief, clarity, and growth. Staying in harm also creates its own regrets.

2. What if they change and I missed my chance?

→ Real change includes accountability and safety. If they change, there's space to re-evaluate. But your boundary today is valid based on who they've been.

3. What if people think I'm cruel or selfish?

→ Not everyone will understand. But protecting yourself doesn't require a permission slip from people who weren't there.

4. What if I am the problem?

→ Self-reflection is healthy. But if you're the only one doing it, that's a sign of imbalance—not guilt.

5. What if I end up alone forever?

→ Estrangement often brings grief—but it can also create space for chosen family and authentic connection.

Use this reframing structure for your own thoughts:

- Write the fear: *"What if...?"*
- Identify the assumption underneath it
- Ask: *Is this true, helpful, or kind?*
- Offer a compassionate reframe

Example:

What if I was too dramatic?

→ *I learned to minimize my pain to stay connected.*

→ *Even if others call it dramatic, I know what I survived.*

Visualization: I am my own safe place

This exercise is a grounding tool to reconnect with a sense of internal safety—especially after triggers, anxious spirals, or family contact.

Steps:

1. Sit or lie in a quiet space. Breathe in slowly, then exhale longer than you inhale.
2. Close your eyes and picture a place that feels safe, calm, and private. It could be real (a room, a beach) or imagined (a forest, a glowing light).

3. Picture *yourself* in that space—not as you "should be," but as you are right now.
4. Surround yourself with warmth, light, or softness. Notice how your body responds.
5. Repeat slowly in your mind:

"I am my own safe place."

"I don't have to be perfect to protect myself."

"I can choose peace, even when fear speaks loud."

Breathe here as long as needed. You can return to this space anytime.

***

Fear is not a flaw.

It is a signal—one that helped you survive an environment where safety was inconsistent or conditional.

But now, fear does not have to drive the story.

It doesn't need to decide what kind of love, peace, or future you get to have.

You are not behind.

You are learning to trust yourself more than the voices that once controlled you.

You are your own safe place now.

Part III. What Was Never Your Fault

You weren't imagining it.

You weren't too sensitive.

You weren't failing—you were adapting.

Part III is about unlearning the lies you were taught to believe about yourself.

Maybe you were the scapegoat—the one blamed for everything that went wrong.

Maybe you were the golden child—praised on the surface but never really seen.

Or the peacekeeper—the one who absorbed everyone's pain so no one else had to feel it.

These roles weren't chosen. They were assigned.

And while they may have helped you survive, they also taught you to disappear.

In this section, we explore what it means to be shaped by trauma responses—not as flaws, but as evidence of your nervous system working overtime to keep you safe. You'll learn about fawning, freezing, and the fog of fear, obligation, and guilt that may still cloud your choices.

We'll also look at emotional flashbacks—those moments when the past hijacks the present—and the internalized patterns that leave you second-guessing your truth, a process often called self-gaslighting.

This isn't about blaming.

It's about recognizing what never belonged to you in the first place—and beginning to hand it back.

The goal of this part is clarity: to see what you carried, why you carried it, and how to begin putting it down.

Let's begin the work of understanding not what's wrong with you—but what happened to you.

9. Family Roles — The Cast You Didn't Choose

Families often assign invisible roles—especially in dysfunctional or emotionally unsafe systems. These roles aren't earned or chosen. They're cast by dynamics like favoritism, silence, control, or unmet emotional needs.

When emotional maturity is lacking in caregivers, children are often forced into roles to stabilize the chaos around them. And even if you tried to break free, the role clung to you—until it became hard to tell where the role ended and you began.

This chapter is about making that invisible script visible.

You didn't choose this role.

You survived it.

Common family roles in dysfunctional systems

These roles often shift, overlap, or rotate among siblings—but the emotional impact is lasting.

Use the following as a personal inventory. Which roles feel familiar to you?

1. The scapegoat

Always blamed, even when telling the truth. Often punished for disrupting the family's denial or silence.

Carries: shame, anger, hyper-independence

Learns: "If something goes wrong, it's my fault."

2. The golden child

Favored for high achievement and loyalty. Praised publicly but loved conditionally.

Carries: pressure, perfectionism, imposter syndrome

Learns: "If I succeed, I'll stay loved."

3. The lost child/invisible one

Stays quiet, avoids conflict, and disappears to remain safe. Often emotionally neglected or forgotten.

Carries: isolation, emotional detachment, fear of visibility

Learns: "If I disappear, I won't be a burden."

4. The peacekeeper/parentified child

Keeps emotional balance, absorbs tension, and often takes on adult responsibilities too soon.

Carries: emotional exhaustion, people-pleasing, chronic self-sacrifice

Learns: "If everyone else is okay, I'll be safe."

5. The mascot/comic

Uses humor to keep things light. Distracts from family pain while hiding their own distress.

Carries: internal chaos, hidden sadness, anxiety

Learns: "If I make them laugh, they won't look too closely."

6. The caretaker

Becomes the emotional or practical support system for others, including parents or siblings.

Carries: resentment, burnout, blurred boundaries

Learns: "I'm only valuable when I'm needed."

7. The rebel/black sheep

Refuses to conform. Often labeled "too sensitive," "dramatic," or "disloyal."

Carries: disconnection, misunderstood truth, anger

Learns: "If I speak the truth, I'll be cast out."

8. The achiever/fixer

Tries to solve or redeem the family's dysfunction through overachievement or control.

Carries: anxiety, pressure, distorted self-worth

Learns: "If I work hard enough, maybe they'll love me."

9. The truth-teller

Sees and speaks the dysfunction. Often scapegoated or dismissed for refusing to uphold the family myth.

Carries: rejection, self-doubt, emotional exile

Learns: "Telling the truth makes me unsafe."

Role reclamation exercise

Once you've identified one or more roles you were cast into, use the prompts below to begin separating the *role* from your *real self.*

Use your personal notebook or journaling app to reflect:

1. *What role(s) did I take on in my family?*
2. *Did I choose that role—or was it placed on me?*
3. *What beliefs did I internalize because of that role?*

   (e.g., "My needs make people uncomfortable," "I have to fix everything," "My pain doesn't matter")

4. *What did this role cost me—emotionally, relationally, mentally?*
5. *What strengths or survival skills did this role give me?*

(e.g., empathy, insight, humor, resilience—even survival roles can hold gifts)

6. *What parts of this role no longer serve me?*
7. *What would it mean to step out of this role and define myself on my own terms?*

You get to rewrite the script now.

You get to reclaim your identity.

Creative prompt: Letter from the role to the real you

This writing exercise helps you gently separate from the role you've been stuck in—without judgment.

Imagine the role writing a letter to *you*. Let it speak honestly. Here's a guided opening:

Dear [Your Name],

I've been with you for a long time. I stepped in when things were uncertain.

I tried to keep you safe by [insert role's function—making you invisible, perfect, funny, responsible].

I know I became part of how you survived.

But I also know how heavy I've become.

You're tired. And you deserve more than what I can offer you now.

I wasn't meant to be forever.

I was your armor—but you don't have to wear me anymore.

If you're ready, you can set me down.

Or we can walk together differently—where you lead, and I follow.

With care,

[The Role]

This letter can be handwritten, typed, spoken aloud, or simply imagined.

It doesn't need to be a goodbye. It just needs to be honest.

You don't have to banish the role.

But you do get to reclaim who you are beneath it.

***

You were shaped by survival—not by failure.

The role you played was never your identity.

You are not the fixer.

You are not the scapegoat.

You are not just the peacekeeper or the overachiever.

You are the one who saw the truth.

And now, you're allowed to become the version of yourself who doesn't have to play a part to be safe.

You're not breaking the system.

You're breaking *free.*

10. Trauma Responses — Fawn, Freeze and FOG

Estrangement doesn't begin with distance. It begins with fear.

Fear that you'll be punished for speaking up.

Fear that you'll be abandoned for setting a boundary.

Fear that love will only be given if you shape-shift, stay silent, or say yes when you mean no.

This is how trauma responses are formed—not just in the face of violence or chaos, but in the *slow erosion of safety*.

This chapter is about the nervous system's survival tools—especially the ones that still live in your body long after the danger has passed. It's about understanding *why you shut down, why you appease, or why you still feel frozen when conflict arises*.

You weren't weak. You were adapting.

Let's meet those responses with respect—and learn how to shift them gently.

Understanding the fawn and freeze responses

We often hear about "fight or flight." But in family systems where fighting back wasn't safe and fleeing wasn't possible, the body turns to two quieter responses:

1. Fawn (appease and comply)

Fawning is the instinct to please, appease, or merge with others in order to avoid conflict or abandonment. It often looks like:

- Over-apologizing, even when you did nothing wrong
- Being hyper-attuned to others' moods

- Saying yes when you mean no
- Avoiding expressing needs or discomfort
- Feeling responsible for everyone else's feelings

Fawning is a brilliant survival skill in families where disagreement equals rejection.

But it comes at the cost of your authenticity.

2. Freeze (collapse and disconnect)

Freezing is the instinct to shut down in order to preserve energy and avoid perceived threat. It can look like:

- Zoning out during conversations
- Feeling emotionally numb or dissociated
- Avoiding decisions, conversations, or planning
- Difficulty moving, initiating, or responding under stress
- Wanting to disappear or "go blank"

Freezing kept you safe when action would've made things worse.

But now, it may block you from feeling fully alive.

Understanding FOG: Fear, Obligation, and Guilt

FOG is a term coined to describe how emotional manipulators maintain control. It keeps you trapped in indecision and shame long after the person is gone.

- **Fear** – "If I say no, they'll punish me."
- **Obligation** – "I owe them because they're my parent."
- **Guilt** – "I'm selfish for putting up boundaries."

Even if your estrangement is years old, FOG can keep you feeling tethered.

The key is to name it—because once you name FOG, you begin to move through it.

FOG tracker worksheet

In your notebook, create three columns titled:

Fear | Obligation | Guilt

Under each column, list situations or thoughts that bring up that emotion. For example:

Fear

- *"If I post about my healing online, they'll find it and lash out."*
- *"If I don't answer the message, they'll escalate."*

Obligation

- *"They paid for my education—I owe them loyalty."*
- *"They're aging. I should be there, no matter what happened."*

Guilt

- *"I missed a family wedding. I feel like I'm the bad one now."*
- *"They say they miss me and I feel horrible—even though they hurt me."*

Then ask yourself for each entry:

- *Is this true?*
- *Is this helpful?*
- *Is this mine to carry?*

This process isn't about dismissing your emotions. It's about giving yourself permission to *reclaim your agency*.

Somatic practice: Butterfly hug

This gentle self-soothing tool helps regulate your nervous system when FOG or trauma responses arise.

How to practice:

1. Cross your arms over your chest so that your right hand rests on your left upper arm and your left hand rests on your right upper arm.
2. Lightly tap your hands on your arms—alternating left and right in a slow rhythm.
3. As you tap, breathe in slowly for a count of 4, hold for 2, and exhale for 6.
4. Repeat a few cycles, allowing your body to soften.
5. You may add a phrase like:

"I am here. I am safe. I am allowed to exist."

This tool helps activate the parasympathetic nervous system—your body's natural calming state.

It's okay if you don't feel instantly better. The goal is not to eliminate the feeling, but to *ground yourself in the present*.

Prompt: When did I shrink to stay safe?

In your journal, explore this:

- *When did I start believing that staying small was safer than speaking up?*
- *What behaviors helped me avoid conflict or punishment?*

- *What parts of me have I hidden to stay accepted—my anger, my creativity, my opinions?*
- *How do I still shrink today, even when the threat is gone?*

You may want to write a short letter to your younger self:

"I see why you went silent. You were brilliant for finding ways to survive. But it's safe to take up space now. We don't have to disappear anymore."

***

Fawning is not weakness.

Freezing is not failure.

FOG is not your fault.

These were the ways your nervous system kept you alive—emotionally, psychologically, and maybe even physically. You don't have to shame the strategies that kept you here.

But now... you get to learn new ones.

Ones rooted in truth, sovereignty, and safety you no longer have to earn.

11. Emotional Flashbacks — When the Past Floods In

Have you ever had a reaction that felt *too big* for the moment—but you couldn't stop it?

Maybe someone raised their voice and your whole body went numb.

Maybe a text message made your heart race like you were under threat.

Maybe you cried after setting a small boundary, then questioned why you felt so shaken.

This might not be overreaction.

This might be an *emotional flashback*.

Unlike visual flashbacks—where people relive images or scenes from trauma—emotional flashbacks flood your body with the feelings from a past experience without any clear memory attached.

Suddenly, you're not just feeling what's happening now.

You're feeling what happened then—as if it's happening all over again.

This chapter is about naming that experience.

So you can *anchor yourself in the present*, even when the past tries to pull you back in.

What is an emotional flashback?

An emotional flashback is a sudden, overwhelming experience of old emotional states—especially ones rooted in trauma, childhood wounding, or chronic emotional neglect.

It may include:

- Intense shame or guilt "out of nowhere"
- Feeling small, stuck, scared, or worthless
- Floods of sadness or rage that don't match the current situation
- Urges to hide, apologize, lash out, or shut down
- A sense of being "young," vulnerable, or powerless

Unlike panic attacks, emotional flashbacks are often silent. They don't always have a clear trigger. But the nervous system remembers.

You may not remember *what* happened.

But your body remembers *how* it felt.

Then vs. now anchor tool

This tool is a grounding script to use when you sense you're in an emotional flashback. It helps remind your nervous system: *I'm safe now.*

In your notebook or aloud, walk through these steps:

Step 1: Notice the shift

- *"Something feels off."*
- *"My reaction feels bigger than the moment."*
- *"My body feels scared, frozen, or flooded."*

Step 2: Locate yourself in time

- *"I am [your current age]."*
- *"Today is [name the date]."*
- *"I am in [name the place you're in]."*
- *"This feeling is from the past—it's not happening again."*

Step 3: Reassure the younger you

- *"You were not safe then, but we are safe now."*
- *"You don't have to handle this alone anymore."*
- *"You get to have boundaries now. You get to rest."*

You can write this down and keep it somewhere visible.

When you feel flooded, read it like a lifeline.

You are not losing control.

You are remembering something your body hasn't yet unlearned.

Body-age awareness: "What age does this feeling belong to?"

Sometimes our emotional reactions come from a younger version of ourselves who never got to finish feeling—or healing.

Try this somatic awareness prompt in your notebook:

- *When I feel this emotion, how old do I feel?*
- *What was happening in my life around that age?*
- *Did anyone validate or respond to me when I felt like this before?*
- *What did I need back then that I didn't get?*
- *How can I offer that now?*

You might discover:

- A 6-year-old who learned to stay quiet to avoid punishment
- A 13-year-old who was blamed for everything
- A 17-year-old who felt invisible in her own home

Once you recognize who's speaking, you can respond with care—not shame.

You don't have to exile these parts of yourself anymore.

You can begin to reparent them—with presence, patience, and love.

Example: Flashback in action

You're texting with a sibling. They bring up your estrangement and say: "You're being dramatic."

Your heart pounds. Your face gets hot. You want to scream, cry, and hide all at once.

You're 34—but suddenly, you feel 10 again.

Back then, whenever you expressed hurt, someone told you you were "too sensitive."

This is an emotional flashback.

You pause. Breathe. Use your Then vs. Now anchor:

"I'm not 10. I'm 34. I'm allowed to be upset. I don't need to explain my pain away."

These moments are hard—but they're also *opportunities for reconnection.*

You get to become the safe presence you never had.

***

You are not "too much."

You are not unstable.

You are not stuck in the past—you're just *learning how to unfreeze from it.*

Emotional flashbacks may not disappear overnight.

But every time you name them, soothe yourself, and stay with the feeling—you're breaking a cycle.

The past will always echo.

But now, *you get to choose what to do with the sound*.

12. Self-Gaslighting — Undoing the Doubt Spiral

It didn't start in your head.

But that's where it lives now.

You replay the moment.

You question your reaction.

You wonder if you imagined it all.

This is *self-gaslighting*—the habit of invalidating your own truth because it was never validated by others.

Maybe you grew up hearing things like:

- *"You're too sensitive."*
- *"That's not what happened."*
- *"Stop making everything about you."*
- *"You're remembering it wrong."*

When you're told often enough that your feelings are wrong, you begin to believe it. You start second-guessing everything—from what you felt, to what you saw, to what you deserved.

Self-gaslighting is not a character flaw.

It's a survival mechanism you developed to stay connected in unsafe environments.

This chapter is your space to notice when it's happening—and begin speaking to yourself with the clarity and care you were once denied.

Worksheet: What I told myself vs. what was true

This simple yet powerful exercise helps you separate the internalized voice of gaslighting from your actual truth.

In your notebook, draw two columns:

What I Told Myself | What Was Actually True

Here are some examples to get you started:

- *"I'm probably being dramatic."* | My reaction makes sense given what I've experienced.
- *"Maybe I overreacted."* | They crossed a boundary I've tried to express before.
- *"I should have tried harder."* | I tried too hard for too long. My needs still weren't met.
- *"They didn't mean to hurt me."* | Impact matters more than intent.

Now complete this table with your own self-talk. Notice how often your inner voice echoes things you were told by people who benefitted from your silence.

You get to challenge that script now.

You get to write your own.

Script: If a friend told me this story...

Self-gaslighting often fades when we take a step back and imagine someone we love in our shoes.

Try this practice:

1. Think of a specific situation you're doubting

Maybe it was a conversation, a confrontation, or a memory that leaves you feeling unsure.

2. Imagine a close friend told you the exact same story

Word for word. Their tone, their pain, their confusion.

3. Then ask yourself:

- *Would I think they were being dramatic?*
- *Would I tell them it was their fault?*
- *Would I ask them to just "let it go"?*
- *Or would I believe them, comfort them, and validate what they went through?*

Your answers are the voice you're allowed to give yourself now.

Reframe: You weren't overreacting. You were overriding alarms.

When you freeze, panic, cry, go numb, or set a boundary—only to later doubt yourself—it's not because you were *wrong*.

It's often because:

- You were taught to minimize your pain
- You weren't believed when you spoke up
- You had to ignore your own signals to stay "safe" or accepted

That's not overreacting.

That's overriding the *alarm bells* your body was ringing—because you learned it was dangerous to listen.

Now you get to choose differently.

You can pause and say:

> *"Something happened, and I felt it for a reason."*
>
> *"I don't need to prove it to anyone else to believe myself."*

"Even if no one else gets it—I do."

That's how self-trust is built.

One validated emotion at a time.

***

You were never too much.

You were never delusional.

You were simply surrounded by people who didn't want to see the truth—because it would've meant changing.

But you see it now.

And that's enough to begin the healing.

Checkpoint 2. Reclaiming What Was Always Yours

You've crossed into a deeper layer of this work.

This checkpoint comes after peeling back some of the most embedded dynamics in estrangement: the roles you didn't choose, the trauma responses that kept you safe, the emotional flashbacks that blurred time, and the quiet voice that wondered, *"Was it really that bad?"*

You've likely uncovered not just pain — but patterns. How you fawned, froze, or minimized to survive. How you shrank yourself, doubted yourself, or silenced yourself — not because you were weak, but because you were smart enough to adapt. And how somewhere along the way, your truth got buried under other people's stories.

This checkpoint isn't about perfect clarity.

It's about *recognizing that you are allowed to trust your perception now* — even if it shakes, even if it still competes with guilt or longing.

You're not imagining the harm.

You're remembering it with the tools you didn't have back then.

And that's not regression — it's power.

Let's pause here and acknowledge the reclamation already in motion.

Progress tracker — Checkpoint 2

Take a moment to gently witness what's shifting — not as a test, but as proof that something inside you is stirring toward truth.

Use your notebook or journaling app for reflection.

1. What do I now understand about my family dynamics that I didn't fully grasp before?

Example: "They needed someone to blame — and I made sense as the scapegoat."

Your insight: ______________________________

2. What trauma response shows up most often for me — and how do I recognize it now?

Choose or add your own:

☐ Fawn (appease, over-agree, placate)

☐ Freeze (numb, shut down, dissociate)

☐ Fight (lash out, over-defend)

☐ Flight (withdraw, disconnect)

☐ FOG (fear, obligation, guilt loop)

☐ Other: ______________

"When I feel unsafe, I tend to: _______________"

3. What moments have I caught myself self-gaslighting lately — and how did I respond differently?

"I almost told myself I was being dramatic... but then I remembered what actually happened."

4. What inner voice is becoming louder — the one that doubts me, or the one that defends me?

"I'm starting to believe my own memory."

"I'm still wobbly, but something in me knows what's true."

5. What beliefs or messages did I absorb in childhood — and which ones am I questioning now?

"That my needs were selfish."

"That silence keeps the peace."

"That being a 'good kid' meant disappearing."

6. What somatic signs do I notice when I'm being triggered — and how do I soothe them now?

Examples: Jaw tension, shallow breath, stomach pain, cold hands.

Soothing practices: Butterfly hug, naming the feeling, grounding touch, walking, safe music.

7. A truth I'm reclaiming, even if it still feels shaky:

"I didn't deserve to be treated that way."

"Their version isn't the only one that matters."

"I get to say what happened to me."

Before you turn the page

You've seen what wasn't yours. Now comes the part where you choose what is.

You've just walked through the heart of the hardest truths — not just what happened, but how it shaped your inner world.

You've named the roles you didn't audition for.

You've learned how your nervous system adapted to survive.

You've started to recognize the ways you silenced your own knowing — and what it costs to keep doubting yourself.

That kind of clarity is a turning point.

Not because everything is suddenly resolved.

But because you're now in a position to ask: What do I want to carry forward? And what do I get to rebuild from here?

The next chapter begins a different kind of work.

Not just understanding the past — but reclaiming your identity, your worth, your voice.

This is where healing starts to feel like becoming — not just surviving.

Let's begin, gently.

Part IV. Building Boundaries, Identity and Protection

Estrangement can take so much—connection, clarity, even a sense of who you are. But in the space left behind, something else becomes possible:

You begin to rebuild.

Not just walls to keep pain out—but boundaries that keep you intact.

Not just protection from others—but a new way of protecting *yourself.*

Not just the loss of family—but the quiet return of your *self-worth.*

This section is about the practical and personal foundations of healing. The tools here aren't theoretical—they're the ones survivors of family rupture return to again and again.

You'll start by unlearning the messages that told you who you were allowed to be.

The voices that called you too sensitive, too angry, too selfish.

Then you'll begin replacing those voices with truths of your own: the identity *you* choose—not the one you were *forced into.*

You'll also explore boundary tools—not just how to say no, but how to *stand by it* without crumbling under guilt. You'll confront cultural narratives that may have taught you that honoring your family matters more than honoring your well-being—and you'll learn how to rewrite that script without shame.

And because protection isn't only emotional, we'll also create space for digital, legal, and social safety—what to do when they won't stop reaching out, or when you're expected to show up at the hospital, the funeral, or the final will.

Finally, we'll speak directly to those who didn't choose estrangement—those who were cut off, ghosted, or punished into exile. Because grief without answers leaves a different kind of wound—and that pain, too, deserves space.

You are not what they said you were.

You're becoming someone far more true.

Let's begin.

13. Rebuilding Self-Worth

It wasn't just the things they said out loud.

It was the way they looked at you when you cried.

The silence after your boundary.

The words they used when you were brave enough to speak.

Over time, those messages become internalized.

You start to believe that your worth is tied to your usefulness, your obedience, your silence.

Estrangement may have started with walking away from *them*.

But healing begins with walking back to *yourself*.

This chapter is about recovering the self-worth that was distorted, suppressed, or never nurtured at all.

It's about learning to believe something radical: *you were never the problem*.

Core belief flip exercise

We all carry core beliefs—deep, often unconscious messages about who we are, what we deserve, and how we fit into the world. In families with emotional dysfunction, those beliefs are often shaped by survival, not truth.

Here's how to begin gently challenging them.

Step 1: Identify the message you inherited

Complete this list with beliefs you internalized in your family system:

- "I am too much."

- "I don't matter."
- "I always mess things up."
- "I'm hard to love."
- "I have to prove my worth."

Step 2: Write the opposite truth

Now write a compassionate, grounded flip of that belief—not a hollow affirmation, but a *healing truth* you're ready to grow into:

- "I am allowed to take up space."
- "I deserve to be treated with care."
- "I make mistakes—and I still matter."
- "Love shouldn't require disappearing."
- "My worth is not earned—it's inherent."

Step 3: Anchor with a statement

Choose one flipped belief and turn it into an *anchor* you can return to:

> *"Even if they couldn't see it, I was worthy all along."*
>
> *"I am no longer available for shame that isn't mine."*

You don't have to believe it *fully* right away. The goal is to begin hearing another voice—your own.

"I am" identity anchors

Estrangement can leave a blank space where your identity used to be—especially if your self-concept was built on roles like caregiver, golden child, or emotional sponge.

This practice helps you replant your roots in truth.

In your notebook, finish the following statements. Return to them whenever you feel lost or unworthy:

- I am learning to trust...
- I am allowed to want...
- I am no longer...
- I am reclaiming...
- I am worthy of...

Example:

- *I am learning to trust that I don't need to earn love.*
- *I am allowed to want peace without permission.*
- *I am no longer available for emotional games.*
- *I am reclaiming my time, energy, and joy.*
- *I am worthy of care, even when I'm not performing.*

Write one statement a day. Repeat it aloud if you can. Let your nervous system feel what it means to be enough—even as you're still healing.

Prompt: What would life be like if I trusted myself?

So many estranged adult children grew up being gaslit, dismissed, or emotionally abandoned. It taught you to question your instincts, edit your needs, and overanalyze every feeling.

But what if you trusted yourself?

In your journal, write about:

- What decisions would feel easier if I believed in my own voice?
- Where do I still seek external permission?

- How would I treat myself if I trusted my memories, boundaries, and intuition?
- What kind of life could I build if my self-worth wasn't up for debate?

You might uncover grief. Or rage. Or hope.

Let all of it come.

This is the start of a new relationship—with yourself.

***

They gave you a version of yourself that was never whole.

One shaped by their fears, their wounds, their unmet expectations.

But you are not who they said you were.

You are someone who made it out.

Someone who is learning to return home—to your own truth, your own worth, your own becoming.

You were never too much.

You were never not enough.

You were always *you*.

And that's who we're finally letting rise.

14. Boundaries That Hold

The first time you set a real boundary, it might not feel powerful.

It might feel terrifying.

You may shake.

You may doubt yourself.

You may hear the echo of a family voice: "How could you do this to us?"

But that discomfort? That fear? That guilt?

It doesn't mean you're wrong.

It means you're doing something *radical*—protecting yourself.

This chapter is about boundaries that don't just get said—but *stay standing*. It's about giving you the words when your voice trembles, the inner compass when old guilt kicks in, and the courage to keep choosing yourself—even when it's misunderstood.

Scripts: What to say when pressured

Sometimes the hardest part of boundary-setting isn't knowing *what* to say—it's believing you're *allowed* to say anything at all.

Use these sample scripts as starting points. Modify them to fit your voice, culture, and context:

When pressured to reconnect:

"I've chosen distance because I need peace, not punishment. That decision still stands."

"I'm not ready to revisit that dynamic. Please respect where I am."

"This isn't about holding a grudge. It's about holding a boundary."

When shamed for going no-contact:

"Estrangement isn't easy—and I didn't do it lightly."

"I don't expect you to understand, but I do expect you to respect it."

"What's best for the family isn't always what's safest for the individual."

When guilted during holidays or milestones:

"I can celebrate my life without reopening a wound."

"Being included shouldn't require me to abandon myself."

"I honor the memory, but I protect my present."

When others try to fix or mediate:

"I'm not looking for someone to fix this. I'm looking to be believed."

"Please don't minimize my experience by rushing to reconcile it."

"This isn't a fight—it's a boundary."

These scripts are not weapons.

They are anchors—especially when the storm of guilt or pushback hits.

No is a full sentence practice

You don't have to defend your no.

You don't have to earn your silence.

You don't have to give people more of yourself than you have.

Examples of boundary statements without justification:

- *"No, I'm not available for that."*
- *"That doesn't work for me."*
- *"I'm choosing something different for my healing."*
- *"That topic isn't up for discussion."*
- *"I'm ending this conversation now."*

Each time you say *no* without padding it with over-explanation, you're strengthening your internal boundary muscle.

It may feel awkward at first—but so did abandoning yourself.

Cultural reframe: Honoring yourself is not dishonor

In many cultural, religious, or collectivist traditions, family loyalty is treated as sacred.

Estrangement can be seen not as a survival tool, but as a betrayal.

Setting boundaries may be framed as *disrespect*.

Choosing yourself may be viewed as *dishonor*.

But here's the truth: *honoring yourself is not dishonoring your roots.*

It is possible to:

- Hold cultural values with pride *and* draw limits around harm
- Respect elders *and* reject emotional abuse
- Grieve what you lost *and* refuse to carry shame for choosing peace

If your culture tells you, *"We don't air dirty laundry,"* remember: silence has never cleaned a wound.

Your healing is not a betrayal.

It's an act of courage that just might free generations to come.

Reflection prompts

Use your notebook or journaling app:

- *What's one boundary I've been afraid to set—and why?*
- *When have I softened a boundary to avoid discomfort or guilt?*
- *What would it feel like to set a boundary and not over-explain?*
- *Where did I learn that protecting myself was wrong—and what am I ready to believe instead?*

***

Boundaries are not walls that shut others out.

They're thresholds that say: *"Only what honors me can enter."*

You may lose people when you set them.

But you'll find yourself in the process.

And that's a trade worth making—every time.

15. Digital, Social and Legal Safety

Estrangement isn't just emotional—it's *logistical.*

When you step back from a family system, especially one that doesn't respect boundaries, you're often left navigating new terrain alone:

What if they text, call, or show up uninvited?

What happens if I get sick? If they do?

Can they still be listed as my emergency contact?

This chapter gives you tools to stay safe—not just emotionally, but digitally, socially, and practically.

Because your healing deserves protection in *every* dimension of life.

Privacy and blocking checklist

Your digital safety matters.

If you're limiting or cutting off contact, here are steps to protect your space across platforms.

On your phone:

- Block numbers (and enable silent unknown caller settings)
- Turn off read receipts and location sharing
- Rename or anonymize sensitive contacts

On social media:

- Block or restrict individuals
- Set your profiles to private
- Limit story/viewing settings (especially for indirect contact)

- Review old shared albums or tagged content
- Disable DMs or friend requests from unknown users

Email and messaging apps:

- Create a separate inbox for legal or necessary communication
- Set up filters to reroute messages
- Block specific addresses in Gmail, Outlook, etc.

Other tips:

- Disable shared calendars, streaming profiles, or shared passwords
- Remove location tags from past posts
- Consider using a VPN if stalking or surveillance is a risk

You are allowed to create digital distance.

You don't owe them access to your healing.

Emergency prep: What if they show up?

Sometimes, estrangement doesn't stop them from trying to find you.

Whether it's an unexpected knock on the door, a run-in at work, or pressure through mutual contacts, it helps to *plan calmly before it happens.*

Create a grounded response plan:

1. **Decide in advance:**

- Will you speak to them?
- Will you call for help?
- Will you walk away?

2. **Practice a short statement** to use if you choose to respond:

- "I'm not engaging. Please leave."
- "I've set a boundary, and I'm not opening this conversation."
- "I need you to respect my decision and walk away."

3. **Inform a safe person or neighbor** of potential contact

- Share your boundaries and ask for support if needed

4. **Secure your home and schedule if applicable:**

- Install cameras or smart locks
- Stagger your routines or vary your locations temporarily

This is not paranoia.

It's preparation that gives you back your *power*.

Medical, legal, and end-of-life considerations

Even after years of no contact, estranged adult children may face unwanted contact or obligations during critical moments—medical crises, funerals, or inheritance disputes.

It's painful. But planning now protects you later.

1. **Medical power and decision-making:**

- Review who is listed as your emergency contact
- Consider naming a health care proxy or power of attorney
- Clarify who *should not* be contacted in a medical crisis

2. **Legal documents to consider:**

- Living will / advance directive

- Durable power of attorney
- Will and beneficiary documentation
- No-contact documentation (if necessary)

3. **End-of-life events:**

- You are not obligated to attend a funeral, even if others expect it
- You may choose to grieve privately, create your own ritual, or do nothing at all
- If inheritance or legal closure requires communication, consider involving a third party or lawyer

In your journal, reflect on:

- *What do I want my safety plan to include—digitally, socially, medically?*
- *Who do I trust to help me uphold those boundaries if I'm unable to advocate for myself?*
- *What would it mean to know I've done what I can to protect my peace—even in the unknown?*

***

Healing isn't just about inner work.

It's about *outer structures* that keep that healing intact.

You have the right to protect your energy.

You have the right to protect your peace.

You have the right to prepare, not because you expect harm—but because you *no longer tolerate it.*

Safety is not selfish.

It's sacred.

16. When You've Been Cut Off

Estrangement isn't always a choice.

Sometimes, it's an exile.

Maybe you were blocked without warning.

Maybe your messages went unanswered, your presence unwelcome.

Maybe your family didn't yell—they just *disappeared*.

Being cut off by people you once tried to love—especially family—leaves a wound that feels both invisible and all-consuming.

You're left holding the grief without the goodbye.

This chapter speaks to that wound.

Not the kind that says "I left to survive."

But the kind that whispers, "Why wasn't I worth staying for?"

Let's untangle that lie.

Let's speak directly to the ache of unchosen silence.

Rejection recovery: "It wasn't about my worth"

When someone cuts you off, especially a parent, sibling, or child, it's easy to assume the worst about yourself.

You might tell yourself:

"I must have been too much."

"They gave up on me because I failed them."

"They must be better off without me."

But most family estrangement isn't caused by a single wrong action.

It's rooted in patterns of avoidance, denial, unhealed trauma, and power dynamics.

Being cut off isn't proof of your unworthiness.

It's often a reflection of the other person's discomfort with your truth, boundaries, or identity.

You don't need to shrink yourself to fit back into their silence.

You don't need to punish yourself to justify their absence.

Try this internal reframe:

"Their choice to walk away does not define my value.

It defines what they were unwilling—or unable—to face."

You didn't deserve to be erased.

You deserve to reclaim your voice.

Letter to your abandonment wound

Sometimes, the only way to process grief without closure...

is to create space for *yourself* to be heard.

In your journal, write a letter—not to them, but to the part of you that was left behind.

You can begin like this:

Dear Abandoned Self,

I know how much it hurt when they disappeared. I know the way you looked at your phone hoping it would ring. I know the nights you cried without knowing what you did wrong.

You didn't deserve the silence.

You didn't deserve the shame.

And you don't have to keep proving your worth to someone who chose not to see it.

You are still here.

Still lovable.

Still enough.

Let your letter end however it needs to: in rage, in grief, in tenderness.

There's no right way to say goodbye to someone who never gave you the chance to speak.

Prompt: What closure do I wish I had?

Estrangement without explanation leaves a vacuum—and it's natural to want something to fill it.

In your notebook, write freely on:

- *What words do I wish they had said?*
- *What questions do I still carry?*
- *What did I want them to understand about me before they left?*
- *What would closure look like—if I gave it to myself instead?*

Closure may not come from them.

But you can still give yourself *understanding*.

You can give yourself *permission* to move forward without an apology.

***

You didn't choose this.

But you *get to choose* what comes next.

You get to love yourself where they left you.
You get to hold yourself in the silence they created.
You get to build a life beyond the absence.

Their rejection was never a mirror of your worth.
Only a reflection of what they weren't ready to face.

You are still worthy.
Still here.
Still becoming.

Part V. Life After the Break

What happens after the rupture?

After the silence stretches long enough to feel like your new normal?

You begin to *build forward.*

Not by forgetting. Not by forcing closure.

But by honoring the truth of your experience while making room for something more:

More stability. More connection. More *you.*

This section of the workbook is about living in the *after.*

The anniversaries that sting. The holidays that feel hollow. The surprise grief that shows up on birthdays or in songs or at the scent of an old perfume.

It's about setbacks that confuse you—when you thought you were past this.

It's about the shame spiral that whispers, *"You should be over it by now."*

We'll reframe those spirals as *part of healing*, not proof of failure.

And when the world feels shaky, you'll come back to the people who help you stay grounded. Not the ones who share your blood—but the ones who share your truth.

Your *chosen family.*

These next chapters are here to remind you:

You don't have to rush to be okay.

You don't have to pretend milestones don't matter.

You don't have to heal in straight lines.

What you *do* get to do—is move forward with your own timing, your own rituals, your own people.

Let's begin again—from right where you are.

17. Milestones Without Family

There's a special kind of ache that comes on the days that *should* feel joyful.

Birthdays. Weddings. Holidays. Graduations.

Days where people assume family will be there—taking photos, giving speeches, sharing tears.

But for you, they come with a quiet grief.

An empty seat. A message you'll never get. A silence that swells louder than celebration.

This chapter is here to hold those days.

Not to fix them.

But to *honor what they stir up*—and help you move through them with preparation, compassion, and rituals of your own.

Tool: Emotional prep for big days

Think of emotional prep like packing a bag before a long trip—not because you expect disaster, but because you know what you *need to feel supported.*

Use the following checklist in the week leading up to a milestone:

1. Identify your emotional forecast

Ask yourself:

- What feelings are already bubbling up?
- Am I anticipating sadness, anger, numbness, nostalgia?

2. Choose your support system ahead of time

- Who can I check in with before or after the day?
- Do I want company, or solitude?

3. Create a flexible plan

- What will I do if a wave of grief hits?
- What can I say to myself when emotions surge?

4. Set boundaries (yes, even with joyful people)

- "Thanks for thinking of me—this day is complicated."
- "I might go quiet. Please don't take it personally."

5. Prepare a "comfort kit" (digital or physical):

- Screenshots of affirming words
- A favorite meal or scent
- A letter from your grounded self to your hurting self
- A playlist, quote, or object that reminds you: *I'm still here. Still safe.*

Grief rituals for anniversaries, holidays, weddings

Ritual isn't about pretending everything's okay.

It's about creating intentional space to *honor what hurts—and what's still meaningful.*

Choose what fits. Let go of what doesn't.

Ideas for private grief rituals:

- **Light a candle** for what you lost, and name it out loud.

- **Write a letter** to the version of you who once imagined this day differently.
- **Create a memory altar** with photos, symbols, or items that feel sacred—even if those memories are mixed.
- **Make a "what I needed" list:**

On this day, I needed... presence, protection, love, space.

They couldn't give it. But I still deserve it.

Ideas for meaning-making alternatives:

- Start a *new tradition* with friends or chosen family
- Donate, volunteer, or create something in honor of your own resilience
- Allow yourself to cry *and* laugh—grief and joy can coexist

You get to write new stories around these days.

You get to decide what celebration and remembrance mean now.

Reframe: "Missing them doesn't mean they were safe"

You might find yourself missing them on these days—and that can feel disorienting.

But missing someone isn't proof they were good for you.

It's proof you're human.

It's proof you once hoped, once longed, once loved.

It's proof you still carry the echoes of the connection you deserved to have.

Try this gentle inner reframe:

> *"I miss the idea of them.*
>
> *I miss the version of family I never had.*

I don't have to rewrite the past to honor that grief."

Missing them doesn't mean you were wrong.

It means something mattered—and it still does.

***

You are allowed to grieve on joyful days.

You are allowed to feel lonely even when you're surrounded by love.

You are allowed to carry absence with tenderness—not shame.

Milestones without family don't have to be empty.

They can become *sacred spaces of self-recognition.*

You made it here.

Even without them.

That's something worth honoring.

18. Triggers and Setbacks

You thought you were past it.

You'd set boundaries.

You felt steady.

Then—suddenly—a scent, a holiday, a name, a song...

And you're back in a wave of grief, shame, or rage.

It can feel like your healing has come undone.

But here's the truth: *what looks like a setback is often a signal.*

A signal that your nervous system is alert.

That a wound is being touched.

That something in you still wants safety, still wants space, still wants care.

This chapter is not about pushing past triggers.

It's about recognizing them as *part of the process*—and equipping yourself to meet them with tools, not judgment.

List: Visual, auditory, digital triggers

Triggers can be sneaky. Sometimes they're loud and obvious. Other times, they're subtle but sharp. Start noticing your patterns.

Visual triggers

- Family photos on social media
- Places tied to painful memories
- Certain facial expressions or gestures
- Seeing people with "close" parent-child dynamics

Auditory triggers

- Tone of voice that mimics a family member
- Songs played during traumatic or emotionally intense events
- Holiday music or religious phrases
- Yelling, silence, passive-aggressive sighs

Digital triggers

- Being tagged unexpectedly in a family post
- Getting a message from a blocked or "no-contact" person
- Seeing their name in an unexpected place
- Comments that say, "But they're still your family..."

Use your journal to jot down your own triggers—big or small. Awareness is the first step in reclaiming your sense of safety.

Plan: "If I see X, I will do Y"

This tool helps you move from *panic* to *preparedness*.

Rather than hoping you won't get triggered, you plan for what you would do *when* or *if* it happens.

Examples:

- If I see a family photo online, I will log off for 10 minutes and do 4-7-8 breathing.
- If I hear that phrase my mother used to say, I will place a hand on my heart and repeat: "That's not my truth anymore."
- If I'm invited to a triggering event, I will check in with my body first before saying yes out of guilt.
- If I dream about them, I will journal one line: "That was then, this is now."

Write your own *If–Then* healing statements in your notebook. These aren't rigid rules—they're grounding reminders that you have a choice now.

Anchoring object exercise

Sometimes when you're triggered, words disappear. You freeze. You dissociate.

That's where anchoring objects come in—a tactile, physical tool that helps bring you back to the *here and now*.

How to use an anchoring object:

1. **Choose something small and comforting**

   A smooth stone. A fabric swatch. A bracelet. A small token. Something with meaning.

2. **Imprint it with a calming intention**

   Before you carry it, hold it and say:

   "When I touch this, I come back to myself."

3. **Use it in triggering moments**

   Reach for it. Hold it. Breathe with it.

   Let it remind you that *you are in a new chapter now*.

You're not powerless to the past.

You're learning how to stay with yourself, even when the old wounds call out.

***

A trigger isn't a failure.

It's a flare from a part of you that still wants to feel seen and safe.

And every time you meet that flare with care instead of criticism, you are rewiring something deep.

You're not going backward.

You're building capacity.

You're learning how to *carry the old pain with new tools.*

This isn't regression.

It's resilience in motion.

19. Healing Isn't Linear

You've made progress.

You've grown, cried, written, released.

And then—suddenly—you find yourself revisiting old pain.

You thought that part was done.

But healing doesn't move in straight lines.

It doesn't check boxes.

It doesn't follow a neat sequence from grief to peace.

Healing moves in spirals.

You revisit old emotions with *new understanding*.

You come back to familiar wounds with *more capacity*.

You relive echoes—not because you've failed—but because your nervous system is learning how to feel safe in places that once terrified it.

Diagram: Spiral of revisited emotions

Imagine your healing not as a ladder with fixed rungs, but as a spiral staircase.

You circle around similar experiences again and again—but each time from a slightly *higher*, slightly *wider* vantage point.

Here's what that might look like:

- Year 1: You cry through the holidays.
- Year 2: You still cry—but you also rest, and prepare.
- Year 3: You light a candle, grieve, and make a new ritual.

- Year 4: You still feel the ache—but it no longer defines your day.

The pain might return. But so does your *strength.*

And this time, you're not meeting it with the same tools—or the same sense of self.

You're meeting it with the person you've become.

Prompt: "What returned — but softer this time?"

Reflection can help us witness our own growth.

Use this prompt in your journal:

What feeling came back recently? What situation stirred up something old?

But this time... how did I respond differently?

What softness, strength, or clarity did I bring with me this time around?

You may notice:

- You paused instead of people-pleased
- You cried, but didn't collapse
- You asked for help, instead of hiding

That is *healing in motion.*

Permission note: "You're still healing, not failing."

Let this be your permission slip:

You don't have to be "over it."

You don't have to be perfect.

You don't have to pretend you've arrived.

You're still healing, not failing.

You are allowed to loop back and feel it again.

You are allowed to revisit.

You are allowed to soften—without erasing your progress.

Some chapters don't close in one sitting.

Some layers peel back slowly.

But every return to the pain is also a return to yourself—

with more wisdom, more tools, more self-trust.

***

Healing is a spiral—one you walk with grace and grit.

Each curve brings a chance to *respond instead of react*.

To soothe what once overwhelmed you.

To love the parts of you that still need time.

There's no final rung.

There's only *next steps*—and you're already taking them.

Checkpoint 3. Witnessing the Spiral

You've looped through some of the deepest emotional terrain in this journey—not once, but many times.

Grief returned in softer waves.

Old triggers whispered instead of screamed.

Boundaries wobbled, but they held.

You came back to parts of yourself that once felt lost—and this time, you stayed.

This checkpoint is here to acknowledge what doesn't always show up in milestones or metrics: *the quiet growth.*

The kind that happens in a pause.

In a decision not to react.

In a moment of self-trust that used to feel impossible.

You're not the same person who began this chapter.

You may still feel fragile.

You may still question the path.

But the spiral has brought you back with *more wisdom, more self-awareness, more tools.*

Let's take a moment to reflect—not on perfection, but on presence.

Progress tracker — Checkpoint 3

Circling back, standing taller

Use your personal notebook or journaling app. Answer honestly, gently, and in your own time.

1. What emotion recently resurfaced—but felt different this time?

Example: "Sadness came back, but it didn't undo me."

Your response:

2. What's one moment in the past month where you caught yourself responding instead of reacting?

Example: "I paused before replying to a message that used to trigger me."

3. What do I know now that I didn't know the last time this feeling showed up?

Reflect on what has shifted in your insight, your body, or your boundaries.

4. What old role or coping pattern tried to return—and how did I meet it differently?

☐ Fawn (appeased or over-explained)

☐ Freeze (withdrew or shut down)

☐ Fixer (tried to solve someone else's emotional mess)

☐ Self-blamer (assumed it was your fault)

☐ Other:

How did you meet it this time? With pause? With truth? With a new boundary?

5. What do I need more of right now—not in the future, but today?

☐ Rest

☐ Affirmation

☐ Silence

☐ Support

☐ Movement

☐ Creative expression

☐ A reminder that I'm not behind

☐ Other: ____________

6. A sentence I want to carry forward from this point on:

"Even if I loop back, I carry more with me each time."

"I'm not broken—I'm building."

"I don't have to be healed to be whole."

Your own sentence: _______________

Before you turn the page

The spiral doesn't always feel like progress.

Sometimes it feels like returning to pain you thought you'd left behind.

But every return brings a new version of you.

A little softer.

A little steadier.

A little more sure that *this time*, you won't abandon yourself.

You've shown up again—for your truth, for your healing, for your becoming.

The next chapter begins the work of connection—not because you've finished healing, but because you've created enough space to invite new forms of love in.

Let's continue—on your terms, in your timing, and with your truth intact.

20. Chosen Family and Real Belonging

Estrangement can make the world feel smaller.

People disappear—sometimes by choice, sometimes by silence.

What's left behind is often not just grief, but *disconnection*.

And yet...

There's a different kind of family waiting to be built.

A family chosen, not assigned.

A belonging rooted in truth, not obligation.

A connection that says, "I see who you are—and I stay."

This chapter is about that rebuilding.

Not rushing into relationships for the sake of filling a gap—but slowly, consciously, creating a circle of safety around your story.

Support map: Who's safe, who's real

It's hard to build connection if you don't know where it already exists.

This tool helps you identify what relationships feel supportive—and what boundaries might still be needed.

In your notebook, create three columns:

1. Safe and supportive people

- Who listens without judgment?
- Who makes you feel more like yourself after you talk to them?

2. Unclear or conditional relationships

- Who is inconsistent, but still in your life?
- Who do you feel "on edge" around?

3. Draining or unsafe connections

- Who leaves you feeling guilted, blamed, or invisible?
- Who do you still perform around out of fear?

Once mapped out, reflect:

- Who could I lean on more intentionally?
- Who needs stronger boundaries—even if I still care about them?

You get to decide who stays close.

Your comfort and safety matter more than obligation.

Script builder: "How I share my truth safely"

When you've experienced family rejection, sharing your truth with others can feel terrifying.

You may fear being too much.

You may fear being misunderstood.

You may fear silence in response.

This script builder offers ways to speak honestly—at your pace, with your boundaries.

Try starting with:

- "There's some complicated family stuff I'm working through. I don't have all the words yet, but I appreciate you being here."

- "I may not talk about my family often—that's intentional. Thanks for respecting that."
- "I come from an experience of estrangement, which means connection looks a little different for me."
- "I value our relationship because I feel safe being real with you."

Use your journal to script what feels true and possible for you.

Remember:

You don't owe your full story to everyone.

You deserve to be met with care—not curiosity.

Tool: 3 go-to people for my tough days

Not everyone in your life can offer the same kind of support—and that's okay.

This tool helps you identify your specific go-to people for moments when you need:

- Comfort
- Practical help
- A grounding presence
- A reminder of who you are

In your notebook, list three people:

Person #1: My soothing voice

The one who listens gently, without trying to fix you.

Person #2: My anchor

The one who reminds you of your values and how far you've come.

Person #3: My "Let's get out of here" buddy

The one who shows up with snacks, humor, or silence—no explanation required.

If you don't yet have three, that's okay.

Let this be a vision board for what you're creating—not a test you're failing.

Reflection prompts

Use your notebook or journaling app:

- What does belonging mean to me now—without the influence of family roles or expectations?
- Who in my life makes me feel emotionally safe—and how do I know?
- When have I felt seen recently, even in small moments?
- What kind of support am I still looking for—and how might I begin inviting it in?
- If I imagined building a chosen family, what would that look and feel like?

***

Estrangement may have taught you what connection isn't.

But you still get to discover what it *can* be.

Chosen family isn't built in a day.

It grows from small moments of trust, tenderness, and truth.

You don't have to do it all at once.

You don't have to do it alone.

Start where you are—by naming what you need and noticing who honors it.

Real belonging doesn't demand perfection.

It welcomes your whole self, exactly as you are now.

PART VI. Your Future Is Still Yours

There comes a time in healing when the question shifts.

It's no longer just "Why did they do this?"

It becomes, "What do I want to carry forward?"

This part of the journey is not about forgetting or pretending.

It's about choosing what to do with what happened.

It's about loosening the grip of the past—not because it didn't matter, but because *you* matter more.

Forgiveness might live here. Or it might not.

Peace might include them. Or it might never.

But the future? That part is yours. Entirely.

In these final chapters, we'll explore your power to define what healing looks like *now*—on your timeline, with your voice, and without needing anyone else's permission to move forward.

You'll reflect.

You'll release.

You'll reclaim.

And whether or not you ever get the apology, understanding, or return you once hoped for—

you'll write a closing that honors your truth.

Because healing isn't waiting for them to say the right words.

It's realizing you already have the ones you need.

Let's move forward—at your pace, on your terms.

You don't need the past to change in order to build something beautiful from here.

21. Forgiveness and Your Timeline

There's a quiet pressure that often creeps into conversations about healing: "You'll feel better when you forgive."

But healing doesn't have a universal formula.

And forgiveness is not the price you have to pay to move forward.

This chapter isn't here to tell you what to do.

It's here to remind you: *you get to define what peace looks like.*

And if forgiveness is part of that—beautiful.

If it isn't—*still beautiful.*

You don't owe healing to anyone but yourself.

And you certainly don't owe forgiveness to the people who hurt you to prove you're "over it."

You get to take your time.

You get to stay in choice.

Forgiveness decision tool: Optional, not required

Let's slow the conversation down.

Before asking "Should I forgive them?" try asking questions that center your safety, not obligation:

- Do I feel safer imagining a future where they remain distant—or involved?
- Am I hoping forgiveness will restore something—or simply free me?
- Would forgiving feel like self-respect—or self-abandonment right now?

- If I choose not to forgive today, can I trust myself to revisit the question if or when I'm ready?

This isn't a test.

There's no moral scoreboard.

What matters is that your answer reflects *your inner compass*, not social pressure.

Write in your notebook:

"Forgiveness, for me, currently means..."

And add:

"I give myself permission to hold that definition loosely."

Prompt: What does peace look like—with or without them?

So much energy can go into imagining what would happen if they changed.

But what if peace didn't depend on them at all?

Reflect in your journal:

- If I never get an apology... what would peace still look like?
- If we never speak again... how could I create a sense of wholeness anyway?
- If I stopped waiting for them to understand... what could I finally turn toward instead?

Peace is not a prize someone else gives you.

It's a process you gift yourself.

Letter to future you

There is a version of you that hasn't been born yet.

A version that's lighter—not because nothing hurts anymore, but because you've learned how to carry it differently.

You don't have to know exactly who that version is.

But you can begin writing to them now.

Start with:

Dear future me,

I don't know how it will all unfold. But here's what I hope you've found...

Write as if they're still becoming. Because they are.

Because *you* are.

Let this be your reminder:

The future doesn't have to look like the past.

It can be shaped with softness. With sovereignty. With self-trust.

***

Forgiveness isn't the finish line of healing.

It's one possible path—and not the only one.

Whether or not you ever choose it, what matters most is this:

You are reclaiming your time, your terms, your *timeline.*

You are not behind.

You are not unfinished.

You are in motion—carving out a future where your needs matter more than *their validation.*

And that...

is already a radical act of hope.

22. Closure Without Their Words

There are stories that end without a goodbye.

Questions that never get answered.

Hurts that were never named out loud.

And yet, somehow, here you are.

Still healing. Still growing.

Closure, for many of us, doesn't arrive neatly wrapped in a conversation or an apology.

It doesn't always come from them.

Sometimes, closure comes from you—

from the decision to stop waiting.

From the moment you choose to name the ending yourself.

This chapter is an invitation to do just that.

Final unsent letter

There's power in writing what you'll never send.

Use this space to express everything left unsaid.

The grief. The rage. The longing. The silence. The truth.

You can begin with one of these openings—or let your voice lead:

- "This is what you never saw..."
- "Here's what it cost me to keep the peace..."
- "I wanted you to love me like this—but you didn't."
- "You don't get the last word. I do."

This letter is not for them. It's for *you.*

You don't need their validation for your experience to be real.

You only need to give yourself the space to be *fully honest*—perhaps for the first time.

Symbolic rituals: Burn, bury, plant

Words alone aren't always enough.

Our bodies and nervous systems often need ritual to mark the ending of something hard.

Try one of the following:

1. Burn — Releasing anger or grief

Safely burn your unsent letter in a fire-safe container.

Watch the smoke rise.

Let the flames carry away what you've carried for too long.

2. Bury — Honoring the death of what was

Place your letter—or even just a note of what you're releasing—into the earth.

Cover it with soil. Let it rest.

This is the burial of what could not be.

3. Plant — Reclaiming what comes next

Plant something new—flowers, herbs, a seed.

As it grows, let it remind you: *endings can still make space for life.*

These rituals aren't about pretending it didn't matter.

They're about reclaiming your power to choose what comes next.

Affirmation page: You are the ending you needed

Take a moment.

Say this aloud—or write it in your notebook.

Let the words settle in your body like a vow.

I may never get the answers I wanted.

I may never hear the words I longed for.

But I am not waiting anymore.

I don't need their permission to heal.

I don't need their understanding to move on.

I get to give myself the ending I deserve.

I am the one who stayed when they didn't.

I am the one who listened when they denied.

I am the one who chose truth when silence was easier.

I am the ending I needed.

And now—

I am the beginning, too.

***

You've come to the end of this chapter.

But not the end of your healing.

Because healing doesn't end.

It evolves.

You've walked through the ache. The absence. The aftermath.

And here, in this moment, you've done something powerful:

You've claimed your story.

You've honored your pain.

You've chosen to close a chapter—on your own terms.

And that...

is everything.

Checkpoint 4. The Ending You Get to Write

You've reached the final checkpoint.

But not the final word.

Not the end of your growth.

Not the end of your story.

This checkpoint is here to witness something powerful:

You stayed with yourself.

Through the rupture.

Through the ache.

Through the silence that wanted to convince you it was your fault.

But here you are—still healing, still becoming.

And that is no small thing.

You've reclaimed memories.

Rewritten roles.

Reconnected with parts of you that once felt exiled.

You've spoken truths no one else may ever validate—and still, you spoke.

This moment is not about what's been resolved.

It's about what's *now* possible.

Because you no longer need someone else to give you closure.

You've chosen to give it to yourself.

You are no longer just surviving estrangement.

You are becoming someone beyond it.

Progress tracker — Checkpoint 4

Integrating Healing, Honoring Wholeness

Use this final reflection not as a test—but as a gentle mirror.

Write freely in your journal or notebook. Be honest. Be kind.

1. **How would I describe myself now—in one sentence or phrase?**

- "I'm someone who chose myself, even when it hurt."
- "I'm learning to live in truth, not performance."
- "My story is mine now."
- Your words: ___________________________

2. **What feels different in my body, my voice, or my boundaries now?**

Notice how your healing has shaped not just thoughts—but your physical, emotional, and relational patterns.

3. **What am I most proud of—not for anyone else, but for me?**

Was it walking away?

Was it staying kind to yourself during a spiral?

Was it finally saying no—and meaning it?

4. **What do I still grieve—but carry with compassion, not shame?**

Write what still hurts—but without judgment.

5. **What truth have I made peace with, even if it's unresolved?**

"I may never understand why they left."

"I'll never get the apology. But I no longer need it to move forward."

6. **What does "moving forward" mean for me now—on my own terms?**

More softness?

More boundaries?

More joy that doesn't need to be earned?

7. **Final prompt: What am I choosing to carry forward—and what do I leave here?**

Carry: ______________________________

Leave: ______________________________

Before you turn the page

You've walked through it all.

The guilt. The anger. The numbness. The doubt. The truth.

You've written unsent letters.

You've sat with rage.

You've questioned your worth—and found your way back to it.

You've said your goodbyes without applause.

You've claimed your peace without their permission.

You've imagined a life that no longer centers their story.

And now, you've reached this page.

Not to end anything—

But to mark a beginning.

You are the closure.

You are the courage.

You are the continuity.

You've come this far.

And the rest of your story?

It's yours to write.

***

Closure doesn't always come in words — but in how you carry yourself forward.

By now, you've moved through every corner of this experience:

The confusion.

The rupture.

The grief.

The rebuilding.

The quiet, sacred act of choosing yourself again and again.

You may still carry questions.

You may still carry love.

But you no longer have to carry the weight of explaining your pain to be valid.

The next section is here to support your continued journey — with scripts, tools, prompts, and language for real-life moments.

You don't have to use everything.

Take what fits. Leave what doesn't.

Return when needed.

Because healing isn't about finishing — it's about finding your own rhythm forward.

Let's keep going, with clarity and care.

The next pages are yours to use as you need them.

Appendix A. Scripts for Real Life

What to say when you shouldn't have to say anything—but you do.

Estrangement doesn't come with a guidebook. And it doesn't stay neatly inside your personal life—it shows up at work, in texts from relatives, at weddings, during holiday potlucks, and especially when someone casually says, "So what are your parents up to?"

That's where this appendix comes in.

These aren't perfect lines, and you don't have to say them word-for-word.

But they *can* give you something to lean on when your voice catches or your nervous system locks up.

Every situation here includes a quick explanation—*why* this moment might feel tricky and *what you can try saying* to protect your peace.

1. When someone casually asks about your parents or family

This is one of those seemingly harmless moments that can take your breath away. Someone asks where your parents live or how you'll celebrate the holidays. They don't know they've landed on a scar.

What you say is up to you—and how much energy or safety you feel in that moment.

Low-disclosure, low-drama

"We're not in touch."

If you want to share gently but truthfully

"It's complicated—we've gone our separate ways."

If you need to move on without answering

"Family is a tender subject for me. Mind if we talk about something else?"

2. When coworkers ask about holiday plans

The assumption that everyone has a "home" or "traditions" can be isolating. You're allowed to protect your story, even in professional settings.

Keep it brief and neutral

"I usually keep it quiet—holidays can bring up a lot for me."

Share what feels true without oversharing

"I don't celebrate with family anymore. I've been creating new ways to make the season feel meaningful."

You're not required to soften your truth for anyone's comfort.

3. When someone says, "But they're still your family..."

This is where social conditioning shows up the loudest. It can feel like someone is invalidating everything you've survived in one sentence. If you're up for it, here's how you can respond with clarity:

Naming the disconnect

"Being related doesn't mean someone is safe or respectful."

Naming your values

"For me, love without safety or dignity isn't really love."

Setting a boundary around the conversation itself

"I've made peace with my decision. I'd rather not re-open it."

4. When you're invited to a family-heavy event

Some events—like weddings, family barbecues, or reunions—can trigger old wounds. You may love the person inviting you, but the setting doesn't feel emotionally safe. You're allowed to say no *without guilt* and without explaining your trauma story.

Kind but clear decline

"I really appreciate the invite. Those kinds of gatherings are tough for me, so I'll pass this time."

Offering another way to connect

"Family settings are hard for me. Could we do something smaller, just the two of us?"

5. When someone tries to guilt-trip you for not reconnecting

This is one of the hardest to navigate. Sometimes people think they're being helpful. Sometimes they just don't get it. Either way, it's not their job to approve your decision.

Setting the record straight, calmly

"I didn't choose distance lightly. It was something I had to do to protect my wellbeing."

For those who keep pushing

"I know it may be hard to understand, but it was a decision made after years of pain and effort. I don't need agreement—I just ask for respect."

When you're done defending yourself

"This is what I need to stay emotionally safe. That matters more to me than being understood."

6. When a friend keeps asking questions you're not ready to answer

Even people who care deeply about you might not realize how exhausting—or invasive—their curiosity can feel. You get to protect your emotional energy.

Gently name your boundary

"That's still something I'm working through privately. I'm not ready to talk about it yet."

If you need to be firmer

"I'm not comfortable discussing that part of my life. I'd appreciate if we could leave it there."

You're not being distant. You're being self-protective—and that's wise.

7. When someone offers advice you didn't ask for

Sometimes people try to fix what they don't understand. They think a suggestion or a quote about forgiveness will somehow make it better. But unsolicited advice often misses the mark—and you're allowed to say so.

Kindly redirect

"I know you mean well, but I'm not looking for advice right now—just someone who can listen."

Set a boundary with clarity

"This is something I've spent a lot of time processing. I'm not open to suggestions about it."

8. When someone suggests reconnecting or "just calling them"

It's painful when someone oversimplifies the depth of what you've survived. "Have you tried calling them?" can feel like a slap. You can protect your reality with as few—or as many—words as you want.

Direct, no explanation needed

"I've already made that decision, and I'm not revisiting it."

Gentle but resolute

"This isn't about a lack of trying. It's about what's best for my emotional health now."

9. When opening up to someone new (dating or friendship)

Opening up about estrangement can feel risky—especially when you don't know how someone will respond. But sometimes, connection deepens when you name your truth.

Start with a soft introduction

"My relationship with family is... non-traditional. It's something I navigate with care."

If you want to offer a boundary with it

"It's not something I share all at once. If or when I do, I just ask for some gentleness around it."

Your story is a privilege—not an expectation.

10. When someone asks why you haven't forgiven or reconnected

You don't owe anyone a philosophical explanation. Forgiveness is personal. Contact is a choice. Healing looks different for everyone.

Simple and honest

"Forgiveness doesn't always mean reconnection. And peace doesn't always include contact."

When you want to reclaim your own healing lens

"I don't hold anger—but I do hold boundaries. That's how I protect my peace."

Or, when you're done being polite

"This isn't up for discussion. Please respect my choice."

***

You never have to trade your peace to make someone else more comfortable.

Your boundaries don't need to be explained to be valid.

Your choices don't need to be defended to be respected.

Your story doesn't need to be shared to be real.

Let these scripts hold your hand when your voice feels far away.

Say less when you need to. Say more when it's safe.

Say *nothing* when you know it's time to walk away.

Appendix B. Safety and Legal Planning

Estrangement isn't just emotional. It can also come with real-world safety considerations—especially if your boundaries have been ignored in the past.

This section isn't meant to cause fear. It's here to *empower you with foresight*. Whether you're navigating low-contact or full no-contact, preparing for unwanted contact, or simply setting up your life in a way that keeps you safe, this guide will help you feel more informed and in control.

You deserve to feel secure—emotionally, physically, and legally.

1. Digital safety basics

Start by securing your digital footprint.

- **Update your passwords.** Use strong, unique passwords for your email, phone, banking, and any devices. Avoid anything they could guess (birthdays, pets, hometowns).
- **Enable two-factor authentication.** Add a second layer of security for emails, messaging apps, and financial accounts.
- **Check your privacy settings.** Review who can see your location, posts, friends list, or tagged content on all social platforms.
- **Review old shared accounts.** Remove access to any shared cloud drives, streaming services, or bank logins you once gave a family member.
- **Use a VPN** when browsing if you suspect they may try to trace your online activity.

You are allowed to be unreachable.

2. Physical safety planning

If you fear being confronted, stalked, or otherwise harassed, this section offers steps to reclaim your physical safety and peace of mind.

If you live alone or are worried about being found:

- Don't share your exact address publicly—even with acquaintances.
- Ask your workplace or school not to share personal information with callers.
- Consider installing a doorbell camera or security system.
- Keep a go-bag with essentials in case you need to leave temporarily.
- Make a trusted friend or neighbor aware of your concerns so they can support you discreetly.

If they show up at your home or work:

- You do *not* have to open the door or engage.
- Call local non-emergency police to report unwanted contact if it escalates.
- Keep documentation (dates, times, screenshots) of any threatening behavior.

Safety doesn't mean you're paranoid—it means you're prepared.

3. Emergency preparation checklist

For those navigating high-conflict family estrangement, some preparation can reduce panic in the moment. Use this checklist to create your plan.

Emotional emergency plan:

- Who will you call if you feel destabilized or retraumatized?
- Do you have a grounding technique ready to use if you're flooded with emotion? (e.g., 5-4-3-2-1 sensory grounding)
- Is there a note you can write to yourself ahead of time for when you're spiraling?

Practical emergency plan:

- Do you have a backup contact for work or school in case of a crisis?
- Have you set boundaries with mutual friends or relatives around not passing on messages?
- Are your legal documents (see below) up to date and protected?

Think of this not as worst-case-scenario planning, but as peace-of-mind planning.

4. Medical and legal planning considerations

Estranged adult children may face complex situations where a parent is hospitalized, dies, or tries to reach out through legal channels. Here's how to take back your control.

Medical considerations:

- You are *not legally obligated* to serve as an emergency contact, next of kin, or decision-maker unless previously designated.
- You can choose your own medical proxy. Make it someone you trust and file the paperwork ahead of time.
- In many countries, you can remove yourself from being listed as next of kin—check your local policies.

Legal protections you may want to consider:

- **Restraining orders or no-contact orders** (if harassment or stalking occurs).
- **Estate planning**—ensure your will names beneficiaries you trust, not default family members.
- **Power of attorney documents**—set clear terms about who makes decisions for you in health or financial emergencies.
- **Digital legacy tools**—choose who will control your online accounts and data if something happens to you.

End-of-life planning:

- Do you want estranged family contacted if you're hospitalized or pass away?
- Are there people you *explicitly do not* want informed or involved?
- Put this in writing and share it with someone you trust—especially if you have no contact with anyone in your family of origin.

5. What if they try to reconnect?

Sometimes estranged relatives will break boundaries after years of silence—through letters, messages, social media, or even by showing up.

Ask yourself:

- Do I want to respond at all?
- What method feels *safest* if I do—email, a written letter, or going through a lawyer?
- What is *my line*? (e.g., threats = legal action; guilt = no response)

You have the right to prepare a firm, pre-written boundary reply in case this happens:

"I am not open to communication. Please respect this boundary. Any further contact will be considered harassment."

Save it. Copy-paste it. Or don't respond at all. *Silence is also a boundary.*

***

Planning doesn't mean you live in fear. It means you *live with clarity*.

You've already had to protect yourself emotionally—this is just the practical side of that same self-love.

You are not "overreacting."

You are being *proactive*.

And that's a deeply courageous thing to do.

Appendix C. Cultural, Religious and LGBTQ+ Support

Estrangement is never one-size-fits-all. If you come from a marginalized culture, minority religion, or identify as LGBTQ+, the pain and complexity of estrangement can carry even more layers—because it's not just about family. It can be about survival. Identity. Safety. Shame. And ancestral expectation.

This appendix holds space for those invisible layers. Your story matters, even if the world hasn't made room for it before.

1. Culture and collectivism: When family is everything... until it isn't

In many cultures, family loyalty is a moral code—not just a preference. Estrangement may be seen as *dishonor*, *rebellion*, or *betrayal of ancestors*. But here's what's true:

- *You can love your culture and still leave harmful patterns.*
- *You can carry forward ancestral strength while breaking cycles.*
- *You are not less worthy because you chose peace over obedience.*

Questions to reflect on:

- *What cultural narratives have I internalized about family loyalty?*
- *What values from my culture still serve me, and which ones do not?*
- *How do I honor my roots while also honoring myself?*

Cultural reframe: *Protecting your peace is not betrayal—it's survival.*

2. Religion, spiritual shame and conditional love

If your estrangement stems from religious rigidity or spiritual abuse, the grief may be twofold: the loss of family *and* the loss of a faith community.

Many survivors report:

- Being told estrangement is a sin or "lack of forgiveness"
- Spiritual threats (hell, karma, damnation)
- Pressure to reconnect as a "test of faith"
- Losing community, rituals, or sacred spaces

Know this: Faith and control are not the same. Conditional love is not divine love. You have a right to reclaim spirituality on your own terms—or not at all.

Try this affirmation:

"My dignity is sacred. I do not need to earn worth through suffering."

Optional journaling prompt:

- *What spiritual wounds am I still carrying?*
- *What would a safe version of spirituality (or none at all) look like for me?*

3. LGBTQ+ survivors: When being yourself was the "problem"

If your estrangement is due to your gender identity, sexuality, or queer identity, this appendix is especially for you. Estrangement may feel like rejection of who you are, not just what you did.

You might be grieving:

- The family you hoped would grow to accept you

- The future where you wouldn't have to choose between love and identity
- The version of you that thought "maybe I can be both safe and seen"

Here's what's real:

- You did not cause the rupture by being true to yourself.
- You were never "too much." You were never "the shame."
- It is okay to build family through community, not biology.

Supportive questions:

- *Where do I feel most accepted for who I am today?*
- *What narratives do I still carry about "earning" love or approval?*
- *What do I want my queer joy, safety, or identity to look like—on my terms?*

LGBTQ+ reframe:

Estrangement may be how your freedom began, not how your story ends.

4. Navigating identity in mixed or immigrant families

If you come from a multicultural or immigrant household, identity and estrangement can clash in unique ways. Family may have sacrificed everything for a "better life," and your boundaries may be seen as rejection of their struggle.

But setting boundaries isn't ingratitude—it's evolution.

You might be holding guilt around:

- Not fulfilling traditional gender or filial expectations

- Choosing therapy or autonomy over silence and endurance
- Speaking up about intergenerational trauma

Questions to gently unpack:

- *What beliefs about duty or family do I want to keep—and which need revisiting?*
- *What emotions do I carry that aren't entirely mine, but inherited?*
- *What does healing look like across generations in my family line?*

Reframe:

Your healing honors their sacrifice. Even if they don't understand it.

***

Whatever your background, your pain is real. You don't need to justify your identity to be worthy of healing. Whether estrangement came *because* of who you are—or because of how deeply you needed to protect that truth—you belong in this healing space.

This workbook was made for *all* estranged adult children.

And that includes *you*.

Appendix D. Myth vs. Reality

Estrangement carries more than grief—it carries judgment, misunderstanding, and stigma. People may project their assumptions onto your story, or you may wrestle with internalized myths that leave you questioning your decisions.

This section exists to gently correct the record.

Each myth listed below is something many estranged adult children have been told—or told themselves. The reframes aren't meant to convince anyone else. They're here to remind *you* of what's actually true.

Let this be a place to breathe a little deeper.

1. Myth: "You only get one family—so you should forgive no matter what."

Reality: Forgiveness is a personal choice, not a moral obligation. And family doesn't lose its ability to harm simply because it's family. Protecting your peace is not a failure to forgive—it's an act of self-respect.

2. Myth: "Estrangement is extreme. You must be overreacting."

Reality: Estrangement is often a last resort, not a first reaction. Most people who walk away have tried everything else first: silence, appeasement, self-blame, tolerance. Leaving isn't impulsive—it's earned clarity.

3. Myth: "You're just holding a grudge."

Reality: Holding a grudge is about bitterness. Estrangement is about boundaries. There's a difference between refusing to let go—and refusing to continue being harmed.

4. Myth: "They're still your parent/sibling—you owe them."

Reality: Blood creates biology, not belonging. You do not owe access to someone simply because of shared DNA. Relationships are built through respect, safety, and reciprocity—not genetics alone.

5. Myth: "You're being selfish."

Reality: Self-preservation is not selfishness. In fact, many estranged adult children were taught to center everyone else at the cost of themselves. Prioritizing your wellbeing is *not a character flaw*.

6. Myth: "Maybe you misunderstood them."

Reality: Even when abuse isn't obvious or physical, it still leaves real wounds. Minimizing your pain doesn't make it any less valid. Your experiences deserve to be believed, even when others refuse to see them.

7. Myth: "But they did their best."

Reality: Effort does not cancel impact. You can acknowledge that someone was struggling—and still hold them accountable for how they treated you.

8. Myth: "If you were a better person/daughter/son/etc., you would've stayed."

Reality: Estrangement is often an act of *courage*, not weakness. It takes strength to walk away from what breaks you—especially when staying would've been more socially acceptable.

9. Myth: "You'll regret this one day."

Reality: Regret may come—and you can still *stand by your decision*. Grief and clarity often coexist. Regret doesn't mean you were wrong; it means you're human, navigating impossible choices.

10. Myth: "You failed in life because you don't have a family."

Reality: You haven't failed—you've protected yourself. Estrangement doesn't define your worth; it reflects a courageous decision to prioritize your mental and emotional health. You may feel hurt or alone at times, but you are whole, and your story is one of strength, not shame.

A gentle reframe to carry forward

You are allowed to choose peace over performance, protection over tradition, and healing over history. Whatever story others may tell about your estrangement—your truth still stands.

Appendix E. Glossary of Emotional and Trauma Terms

This glossary is here to name the things you've felt but maybe didn't have words for. Estrangement carries not only grief, but also emotional states shaped by trauma, survival, and self-protection.

Understanding what's happening inside you doesn't mean labeling yourself—it means *validating your experience*. Let this section serve as a gentle guide to the inner world you're learning to honor.

Abandonment wound

The deep emotional pain caused by being rejected, neglected, or emotionally unavailable—often by a caregiver or family member. It can trigger intense fear of being alone or unworthy of love.

Example: "When they stopped responding, it felt like I didn't matter anymore."

Ambiguous loss

A type of grief that occurs when someone is physically present but emotionally unavailable—or physically gone but still emotionally present. Estrangement often creates this kind of unresolved, confusing grief.

You lost them, but not in a way the world recognizes.

Attachment injury

A rupture in your sense of emotional safety, often caused by betrayal, rejection, or neglect in close relationships. These injuries can make future trust or vulnerability feel risky or unsafe.

Healing isn't just about moving on—it's about learning to feel safe again.

Body-age awareness

The understanding that certain emotions or reactions may come from a younger version of yourself—especially if the original wounding occurred in childhood.

Ask: "What age does this feeling belong to?"

Cognitive dissonance

The mental tension you feel when your beliefs conflict with your reality. For example: "They say they love me, but they hurt me." It can lead to confusion, guilt, or self-blame as you try to make sense of opposing truths.

Complicated grief

A prolonged, intense mourning period that doesn't follow the "usual" grief trajectory. Often found in estrangement, especially when there's no closure, recognition, or support.

There's no funeral for a parent who's still alive but gone from your life.

Emotional flashback

A sudden, overwhelming emotional state that pulls you back into the feelings of a past trauma—even without conscious memory. You might feel shame, fear, or panic and not know why.

This is not overreacting. It's your body remembering.

Family roles in dysfunctional systems

These roles often form unconsciously in families where emotional safety is missing. Many estranged adult children will recognize themselves in more than one.

1. **Scapegoat**

Blamed for the family's problems. Often the most emotionally honest member—but labeled as "difficult," "rebellious," or "too sensitive."

They turned the mirror on you so they wouldn't have to look into it themselves.

2. **Golden child**

Idolized and expected to succeed or uphold the family's image. Often used as proof that "nothing is wrong here." Carries the pressure of perfection and conditional love.

Being favored isn't the same as being seen.

3. **Lost child**

Emotionally invisible. Often retreats inward, avoids conflict, and suppresses needs to avoid becoming a problem.

Not being hurt directly doesn't mean you were safe.

4. **Hero**

The over-functioning fixer, high-achieving, and often praised. Seen as the one who "has it all together," even while emotionally neglected.

You were too busy saving everyone else to be saved yourself.

5. **Mascot**

Uses humor or charm to defuse tension and distract from pain. Often hides deep sadness or anxiety beneath a "lighthearted" persona.

You made them laugh so they wouldn't make you cry.

6. **Caretaker/parentified child**

Takes on adult roles far too young—emotionally, physically, or even financially. Feels responsible for others' well-being, often neglecting their own.

You learned to meet needs, but never to have your own.

Fawn response

A trauma response in which you try to appease or please someone to avoid conflict or harm. Common in emotionally unsafe family dynamics.

You go quiet. You apologize too much. You try to make them feel better, even when you're hurting.

FOG (Fear, Obligation, Guilt)

A cluster of emotional levers that keep people in toxic or abusive relationships. Often weaponized by manipulative family members to keep you compliant.

"If you loved me, you'd call more." "After everything I've done for you..."

Gaslighting

A form of emotional manipulation in which someone makes you doubt your reality, memories, or perceptions. Over time, it can make you question your sanity and self-trust.

"That never happened." "You're too sensitive."

Grief reprocessing

The act of revisiting and working through loss with new context, language, or tools. In estrangement, grief often needs to be rewitnessed—especially if it was invalidated the first time.

Inner child work

A therapeutic approach focused on connecting with the younger parts of yourself that were wounded, silenced, or neglected. Helps rebuild self-worth and emotional safety.

Low contact/modified contact

A relationship strategy where you reduce interaction with a toxic or harmful person to protect your mental health.

This is a boundary, not a punishment.

No-contact

A decision to fully cut off communication with someone who has been abusive, unsafe, or unwilling to change. Often made for survival, not spite.

You're allowed to choose peace—even if it disappoints others.

Parentification

When a child is forced to take on adult emotional or caregiving roles—like managing a parent's feelings or responsibilities. This robs children of a secure childhood and creates lifelong hyper-responsibility.

Reparenting

The act of giving yourself now what you didn't receive then: nurturing, protection, compassion, and structure.

"What would I have needed at 7, 14, or 22?"

Self-gaslighting

When internalized doubt, guilt, or trauma causes you to dismiss your own emotions or memories.

"Maybe I'm being too dramatic." "Maybe I made it up."

This is often a survival habit learned from chronic invalidation.

Trauma bond

A strong emotional attachment formed through cycles of abuse, manipulation, and intermittent affection. It can make leaving feel impossible—even when you know it's harmful.

Triggered

A strong emotional reaction (fear, shame, rage, panic) caused by a reminder of past trauma. Triggers can be sensory (a smell, voice, holiday), emotional (a tone), or situational (a phone call, boundary push).

Being triggered is not weakness—it's your body trying to protect you.

Vicarious guilt

The guilt you carry not for something you did wrong, but because others told you their pain was your fault. Common in family systems where shame is used to control behavior.

This is not yours to carry.

Window of tolerance

The optimal emotional range in which you can function and cope. When triggered, you may leave this window—into fight/flight (hyperarousal) or freeze/numbness (hypoarousal).

Learning how to return to that window is a skill. And you can learn it.

***

You don't need to memorize these terms to heal. But sometimes, naming what you've been through helps you stop blaming yourself for how you coped.

Let this glossary be a quiet place of clarity when confusion clouds your path.

Appendix F. The Language of Healing

When words fall short, symbols often speak.

They give shape to what we've lived through — and what we're still growing into.

These images may have appeared throughout your journey in this book: as metaphors, prompts, or quiet anchors. Each one carries meaning. Each one offers a way to see your healing, not just name it.

You don't need to use them all.

Just notice which ones stay with you.

Let them become part of your inner language — reminders of how far you've come and how gently you get to keep going.

The spiral

Healing doesn't go in straight lines.

You may return to the same emotions again and again — but with more awareness, more softness, and more choice each time.

The spiral says: *This isn't backtracking. It's deepening.*

The door

Sometimes doors close — by choice or by force.

You don't have to keep knocking to prove your worth.

Some doors aren't meant to open again. And that doesn't make you unforgiving — it makes you self-protective.

The door says: *Closure doesn't always come from them. It can come from you.*

The anchor

You are allowed to ground yourself in what's true — even when others deny it.

An anchor doesn't stop the storm. It keeps you steady within it.

The anchor says: *You know what happened. You know what hurt. That truth is yours to hold.*

The fire

There are things you've had to let go of — not because you didn't care, but because they kept burning you.

Letting go isn't weakness. It's survival.

The fire says: *You get to burn what no longer belongs to you — and rise from what's been lost.*

The seed

Estrangement is an ending. But it can also be a beginning.

Every boundary planted is a seed. Every act of self-compassion, a sprout.

The seed says: *Even if no one sees your growth yet — it's still happening.*

The mirror

You were never too much.

You were never not enough.

You were just surrounded by people who couldn't reflect you clearly.

The mirror says: *You get to see yourself now — not through their distortion, but through your own clarity.*

The silence

Not all silence is empty.

Sometimes, it's a boundary. Sometimes, a pause for breath. Sometimes, the only safe option.

The silence says: *You don't have to fill every quiet space to prove you're okay.*

The light

It doesn't have to be bright to be real.

Sometimes it's a flicker. Sometimes a memory. Sometimes a future you can't see clearly yet, but feel your way toward anyway.

The light says: *You're still here. Still moving. Still worthy of peace.*

Reflection invitation:

- *Which of these symbols speaks to you most right now — and why?*

You can carry it in your journal, draw it in the margins, or return to it when words are hard to find.

Let your healing speak in its own quiet language.

Appendix G. Letters You Will Never Send

A space to write what couldn't be said out loud

Estrangement often leaves behind words that were never spoken—not because they didn't matter, but because they didn't feel safe. These letters aren't meant to fix or reconcile. They're for you.

Whether you chose distance, were cut off, or carry grief from a fractured sibling bond, the pages that follow offer gentle starting points. Let them be doorways to healing, not pressure to repair.

Letter example 1: For the one who chose distance

Writing to a parent you chose distance from

Dear Dad,

This isn't a letter asking for anything.

It's not a plea, and it's not an apology.

I just need to say the things I never got to say—the ones I swallowed for years to keep the peace.

I tried to be the version of me you could love. Quiet. Grateful. Low-maintenance.

I bent until I didn't recognize myself anymore—until I couldn't tell where your expectations ended and I began.

You may never see it the way I do.

You may always think I'm overreacting or ungrateful.

But what happened between us left marks.

And stepping away wasn't about punishing you.

It was the only way I could stop punishing myself.

I still think about you.

I still wish things had been different.

But I'm learning now that love shouldn't come at the cost of self-abandonment.

This isn't about blame anymore.

It's about release.

You don't have to understand.

But I had to choose myself.

[Your Name]

Letter example 2: For the one who was cut off

Writing to an estranged child or sibling who stepped away

Dear [Name],

I don't know if you'll ever read this.

I don't even know if you'd want to.

But I need to say it anyway.

When you walked away, I didn't understand.

I still don't fully.

At first, I felt angry—like I had been erased.

Then I felt ashamed—like maybe I failed in ways I didn't even see.

I've spent a lot of time thinking about what I missed.

What I said, or didn't say.

What I minimized.

What I refused to look at because it made me uncomfortable.

I know this letter can't undo anything.

And I'm not writing it to fix or force a return.

I'm writing it because I love you.

And I'm learning that real love means giving you space, even if it breaks my heart.

If you never want to talk again, I will honor that.

If someday you decide to reach out, I will be here—not to defend who I was, but to do better if you ever let me try.

I miss you.

And I hope your life brings you peace, even if I'm not part of it.

[Your Name]

Letter example 3: For a sibling

Writing to a sibling who stayed silent—or stood with them instead of you

Dear Sister,

I didn't think it would be you.

You were supposed to be the one who understood.

The one I didn't have to explain everything to.

The one who saw what I saw—who knew how it really was in our family, even when no one said it aloud.

But somewhere along the way, we stopped being on the same side.

Maybe you didn't mean to take their side.

Maybe it wasn't even about sides for you.

But every time you minimized what I went through... every time you rolled your eyes or changed the subject or stayed silent while I was unraveling...

It felt like you picked them over me.

I've replayed it in my head a thousand times:

If I had said it differently.

If I had waited.

If I had swallowed a little more and spoken a little less.

But it's not about one moment.

It's about all the moments you looked away while I was trying to survive.

This isn't revenge.

It's not a grudge.

It's grief.

Grief for the relationship I thought we had.

Grief for the sister I still sometimes wish I could call.

If one day you ever look for me, I hope it's not to argue.

I hope it's to see me—not who I used to be, not who they said I was—but me.

And if that day never comes, I still wish you peace.

[Your Name]

Letter example 4: Letter to my younger self

For those who carry inner child wounds

Example Letter:

Dear Little Me,

You didn't deserve to carry all of that.

The silence. The confusion. The way you had to become small just to feel safe.

You were never too much — they just couldn't hold what you felt.

You asked for love in the only ways you knew how. And when it didn't come, you blamed yourself.

But I see you now.

And I'm so sorry you had to wonder if it was your fault.

It wasn't. It never was.

You didn't imagine the hurt. You just didn't have the words for it yet.

You didn't ask for the roles you were put in — the peacemaker, the overachiever, the invisible one.

You were just trying to be enough.

But sweet one... you already were.

You still are.

I'm here now.

I'll listen.

I'll protect.

I'll never shame you for needing too much or feeling too deeply.

You were always worthy of gentleness.

And I'm learning how to give that to you — one small step at a time.

Love,

[Your Name]

Letter example 5: Letter to my future self

For those still healing and growing forward

Example Letter:

Dear Future Me,

I hope by the time you read this, the ache has softened.

I hope you're surrounded by people who get you — the real you — not the one you had to perform.

I hope you laugh more. Sleep better. Feel peace without scanning the room for danger.

I hope boundaries come easier.

I hope love feels safe.

But if some days still feel heavy... that's okay too.

I want you to remember how far you've come.

How many cycles you broke. How many nights you comforted yourself.

How often you chose healing over silence, even when no one saw.

You didn't have a roadmap — just courage and self-trust built inch by inch.

If you're ever doubting again, reread this:

You made it through things that could have hardened you... and still chose softness.

I'm proud of you.

Keep going.

Love,

The You Who Started It All

Final Word from the Author

To the one who kept turning the page...

You made it here. Not just to the end of a workbook, but through the weight of things most people never see.

You showed up for your healing — not all at once, not perfectly, but honestly.

And that matters more than you know.

Estrangement carves deep and quiet wounds. It leaves grief without funerals, love without language, and questions that don't always come with answers. But you chose to face those wounds, name what was once unnamed, and create a path where none was offered.

That's courage.

You didn't have to become someone else to be worthy of peace.

You didn't have to earn closure from people who couldn't offer it.

And you never needed anyone else to call your healing valid.

You just needed space —

to breathe, to unravel, to reimagine who you are without their story written over you.

If this book held that space, even a little —

if it helped you feel seen, or softened the ache —

then it's done its job.

Wherever you go from here, carry this with you:

You get to write your own ending.

And you are already living proof that healing is possible — even when it's quiet, even when it's slow.

Thank you for letting me walk beside you in these pages.

Amber Zahra

One Voice Helps Another Find the Way

This workbook was written for the spaces that often go unspoken—the grief that doesn't fit into words, the guilt that lingers long after the decision, the ache of missing people who were never really there for you.

If any part of this book helped you feel more seen, more grounded, or more empowered in your healing, thank you for walking this path with courage.

Your voice matters more than you know.

Many adult children navigating family estrangement hesitate to pick up a book like this—until they read a review from someone who's been there. Just a few honest lines can help someone else feel understood enough to begin their own healing.

If there was a page, a reflection, or a tool that gave you clarity, comfort, or even just a moment of peace—I invite you to share that experience.

You can leave a review by visiting your Amazon Orders page, finding this book, and clicking "Write a customer review."

Your words might be the reason someone else feels brave enough to start.

Thank you for reading, reflecting, and honoring your truth.

Thank you for giving yourself the care you may never have been given.

Even small steps forward matter.

With care,

Amber Zahra

About the Author

Amber Zahra writes for those carrying invisible wounds—especially the ones left by family. Her work is for anyone who's been dismissed, gaslit, or told to shrink their pain into silence in order to belong.

Grounded in trauma-informed care, emotional clarity, and research-informed guidance, Amber's books offer support for adult children navigating complex relationships, grief without closure, and the quiet courage it takes to choose distance.

Through a blend of narrative storytelling, psychological insight, and practical healing tools, she creates books that speak to the spaces many of us inhabit: between guilt and self-trust, between loyalty and self-preservation. Her approach integrates evidence-based practices—cognitive behavioral techniques, somatic tools, mindfulness, nervous system regulation, boundary-building strategies, journaling, and reflective prompts.

Her books are for those who haven't always felt seen by traditional self-help. Each one is crafted to offer not just tools, but recognition. Not just strategies, but space.

Amber's readers describe her work as steadying, validating, and deeply human. Whether you're grieving a parent who is still alive, reclaiming your voice after years of silence, or untangling the guilt of choosing yourself, her books are here to meet you—exactly where you are.

To explore more of her work, visit:

amazon.com/author/amberzahra

or scan this QR code

Printed in Dunstable, United Kingdom